Silent Majority

Silent Majority

Women,

Independents, and

Governing

John Marshall

VIP LLC · 2015

Library of Congress Cataloging-in-Publication Data
Marshall, John
Silent Majority: Women, Independents, and Governing
p. cm.
ISBN 0-988-29200-9
1.Women-Politics-United States-History- 20th and 21st Century.
2.Independents-Politics-United States-History-21st Century.   3.
United States Government-Political Reform-History-21st Century.
4.Bureaucracy- Reform-United States Government-History-20th
and 21st Century.   5. Political conflict-United States-History-20th
and 21st Century.   I. Title

2012948474

Printed in the United States of America

Third Edition-2015

Village Idiot Productions, LLC
Box 231
Hot Springs, Montana 59845
vipbigsky.com

9 8 7 6 5 4 3 2 1

For everyone who enjoys and strives for liberty and equality.

Contents

Acknowledgements

In acknowledgment of everyone who is presently in my life and those who have come and gone in my life, living and deceased. All of those people and places who, collectively with their influences, good or bad, contributed to the ideas expressed in the following pages. The tip of the iceberg for artistic influence: Albert Einstein, Frank Zappa, Rahsaan Roland Kirk, A.A. Gill, Norman Mailer, Taki, Mike Royko, Tom Wolfe, Lewis Lapham, Mark Reisner, Steve Roth, Carl Sagan, Leslie Jackson, Neil Young, Judy Gordon, The Marx Brothers, many of the writers over the last three decades at *Barron's, The Speccie, The Times of London, The Economist, The Christian Science Monitor, and The Guardian,* among others, Joan Miro, Captain Beefheart, Charna Halpern, Ornette Coleman, Ann Linquist, Garry Wills, Guy Murchie, and well, enough of that.

Copy editing by Louise McMillin. Editorial assistance from Marcia Aronow and Heidi Gjefle. Publishing assistance from the folks at Lightening Source, and the folks in the Pages division of Apple technical support.

Introduction

Words, once they are printed, have a life of their own - Carol Burnett

Women, politics, and riding waves are three things in life I love. This book is about all three. Women, you can't live with them, you can't live without them, and you can't out shop them. They win three out of three every time. Sadly however, we seem to think it is okay to live without them politically. Here they are over half of the population, now the majority of the workforce, but embarrassingly for the country, under twenty percent of our federal legislators, and only three of the U.S. Supreme Court seats are held by women.

Politics? A nation that started out with 13 states, roughly four million people, mostly of British descent, and two infant political parties, has blossomed into 50 states, with over 300 million people of many races and cultures. As a result the country has now outgrown the two-party system. A two-party political system that is doing more to hinder and cripple the growth of America's version of democracy than help it blossom further. Two parties may have been enough to define a people over 200 years ago, but they cannot even begin to express the thoughts and dreams of Americans today.

About those waves I like to ride, here are two I have my eye on now. The first being the wave of women claiming their place in this country, in small towns like the ones I live near, and large cities where most Americans live these days. In 2010 they became the majority of the workforce for the first time in U.S. history[1]. That isn't enough for them. They now exceed men in entering and graduating from college. Women now hold more college degrees than men. This isn't a fad. It is a wave that is building in size and strength with each passing year.

The second wave is the wave of Americans who have said goodbye to the Democrats and Republicans. Forty percent of voters in this country now call themselves Independents compared to the 31 percent and 27 percent that call themselves Democrats and Republicans, respectively.[2] For Independents, that is up from 33 percent in 2002. At the rate this wave is moving, in 20 years, Democrats and Republicans combined will be less than half of the electorate in this country. Those citizens calling themselves Independent voters are showing anyone paying attention during the last two decades, that Americans continue to show their disgust for both parties by leaving them.

These are two enormous waves; cultural and political tsunamis. Like any tsunami wave, from the surface they don't look like much rolling across America's cultural political ocean. Deeper down, however, they are powerful and unstoppable. Imagine if these two powerful waves, women and Independents merged into one massive wave. The size and strength of this would be something to behold. Could it happen? Of course it could. Much of the world still considers us the land of what Germans call, "unbegrenzt Möglichkeit," unlimited possibilities. We are still that, regardless of what the doomsayers and sourpusses, also known as Punditzes, might say to the contrary.

---

[1] The Economist, Leaders, We did it!, January 2, 2010, p. 7.

[2] McTague, Jim, Republicans Take Your Seats, Barron's, April, 12, 2012, page 20.

In getting started with all of this, Chapter One will address some of the modern misconceptions that permeate our daily political and cultural lives. Misconceptions that have contributed greatly in keeping women and Independents from gaining greater political power, including continued actions by the two major parties to stymie competition. Going forward from there, Chapter Two will highlight some further examples of how the two major parties work together to limit political competition, creating a literal monopoly on the state and national levels, and the behind the scenes influence that funds most of it. Then continuing in Chapter Three, why women, independent of Democrats and Republicans in government represent a realistic opportunity to break the two-party habit. Further still, why Independent women in equal numbers as men in the judicial and legislative branches of state and national government will enhance the national security, domestic stability, and economic growth of the nation.

From there, in Chapter Four, once women help break that nasty two party habit, outlining a way to reform bureaucracy from its many millennium old ways to one that more accurately mirrors our young democratic ideals. Chapter Four is also dedicated to the elected official you love to loathe, whoever they may be, with their incessant talk about cutting spending, and balancing a budget, but never do. Chapter Five starts off by addressing why many of the ideas about women having equal political power expressed in this book are really bad ideas, and ending with the thoughts of former Supreme Court Chief Justice John Marshall on the subject of women in America. The Epilogue is added to the 2015 edition

About that second wave mentioned on the previous page, don't count on getting a surf report any time soon from your favorite Punditzes on the radio or the tube. They are too busy sunning themselves on the beach of celebrity, the "It's All about Me Beach," to care about a distant wave that presently doesn't look like much. Why should they care? Independents don't spend hundreds of millions of dollars on political advertising in an election year the way Democrats and Republicans do. In the minds of the paymasters of our celebrity addled media darlings, no money, equals no existence, equals no news; hence why you hear, read, or see so little about the largest bloc of voters in the United States today. In my mind this is the clearest indication, at least in the realm of politics, modern media has been even more corrupted by the influence of large amounts of cash than the political class they heap scorn on for doing the same.

 Don't expect any better from the majors on the web. They, too, think celebrity beach is the place to be, and they've mostly morphed into an echo chamber of the major media, miming the partisan chant of the two-party system. That means we in this country can forget about the partisan Pundirazzi of TV, radio, or the Net being there to keep us up to date on the strengthening wave of Americans wanting out of the Democratic and Republican stranglehold on our political system. Realize when I use the words Democrat and Republican, I am not referring to the everyday voter, I'm speaking of those self-anointed few, in the upper echelons of the parties, who dictate the policy everyone else in the party must follow. More on that later.

   What would inspire a man to write about women and Independents? Simple: they are all around me in many ways, and can't help but be noticed or taken for granted. Even though I live in a part of the country few urban residents have ever heard of, let alone care about. The things going on here reflect culturally and politically what is happening in the cities.

 This is the western edge of Montana. The state that saw fit to elect the first woman to the United States Congress in 1916.

Congresswoman Jeanette Rankin was typical of women of the state. She was no nonsense, matter of fact, when necessary she spoke her mind unflinchingly in what she believed, and always in pursuit of the reality of the times not the falsehoods. This is the edge of the state that saddles up next to the Idaho Panhandle. It is Lincoln, Mineral, and Sanders counties. It is GRD (Get 'er Done) country, smoke a pack a day country, and we're not talking about the number of cigarettes you inhale, but the number of wolves you can nail. This is cattle country, logging country, mining country, and Ursus horribilis country.[3]

Part of the country where the wildlife just may outnumber the human inhabitants. A place where so many mountain ranges have been created by so many faults, it's hard to tell whose fault it is. It's that part of America when Christmas mass is held, Baptists, Catholics, Lutherans, Presbyterians, and Seventh-day Adventist come together in the same church to celebrate. Where church isn't just about religion, it's about community.

This is a place where girls are outsmarting the boys almost every year two-to-one, and sometimes three-to-one when it comes to graduating from high school with the highest honors. The same way girls are 70 percent of the recipients of the Nordstrom Scholarship Awards for high school students in urban America.[4]

It is a place where the citizens of Lincoln and Sanders counties voted to end partisan elections for all county elected positions. Two of the five counties, in the last 10 years, in Montana to do so. All around me women and Independents are making themselves known by their actions in pursuit of two of America's most cherished freedoms, liberty and equality. The liberty to excel in education regardless of gender and being considered equal to

---

[3] No, not mama grizzly Sarah Palin, the real grizzly bears.

[4] Nordstrom advertisement, New York Times, January 22, 2012, Sec. 1, p. 14-15.

males in being smart enough, and good enough, to pursue any path in life. The liberty to vote for a person with no party affiliation in an election, and in doing so putting all candidates on equal ground, equal footing in the eyes of all who vote.

It is that kind of place on a warm autumn Sunday afternoon when for no reason at all I decide to look outside while reading the Sunday paper, and there it is. That, "It" being a large animal sprinting furiously in my direction from a quarter mile away. In less time than it takes to exhale comes the realization that this is a buffalo. The instant my shocked brain registers that thought, this buffalo launches himself over a four strand barbed wire fence and clears it with ease. Now he's on my side of the fence and blazing at such a pace that his hooves are sending shards of earth skyward in their wake. His speed beggars belief and as he draws nearer, heading in a northwest direction, I can see the flared nostrils devouring the afternoon November sky. Eyes wide white with a maniacal look of an animal possessed with what I can't begin to fathom.

As he flashes by, my eyes follow, and into my view I spy the object of his lunatic stampede. A herd of cattle being pushed along the road. A modern day cattle drive complete with four wheeled horses named Honda™, Suzuki™, and Yamaha™.

This maniacal buffalo is chasing his adopted herd being marched down the lane and now sprinting west on my side of the fence trying to catch his domestic soul mates. The sprinting stops instantly once he meets the corner of the fence line. From a standstill Mr. Buffalo launches over another chest high fence and rockets down the road after the herd. I have just witnessed nearly a ton of bones and muscle leap over not one but two fences, cover over half a mile, and do it in the same time it takes to drink three sips from a cup.

I decide to walk down the fence line to see if any damage has been done, and following the hoof prints in the grass until I come upon the spot of the second leap. Nothing, not even a wisp of fur in the wire. While walking back to the house I start to realize, in the not so distant past, this scene played itself out again and again   farther east on the prairie. Instead of one buffalo it was millions doing the same thing, same blinding speed, and same maniacal look. Back then it shook it earth. I realize, too, why grizzly bears can reach 35 mph in a sprint. How else could you catch a bigger, wilder, and faster ancestor of my leaping, sprinting neighbor?

Speaking of which, my next door neighbor Randy drives up. Obviously bemused by what has taken place, and asks,

"How's it going?"

"Oh, the usual BS." I reply.

"Usual BS?"

"Yeah Randy, buffalo Sunday."

He starts to chuckle and, being Randy, his whole body chuckles with him. Then along comes a smile on his face that is as full as the Big Sky horizon is wide.

That's how Sundays can be around here.

The same way Sundays mean the grocery store is closed because, well, it's Sunday and what's wrong with taking a day off from shopping? This is also part of the country, like much of rural America, where the original strains of self-governing laid out centuries ago by the founders of a new nation are still active and visible. In some ways not as intended by manifesting as sprouts of vigilanteism, distrust of government, and distain for the law. Mostly though, of cooperation, of getting along to help ones neighbor or members of the community.

Where the phrase, "It wouldn't be right," is the unwritten law people here have followed for generations. Where if you wanted to just go out and hunt on some nearby private land without asking the owner, or not to fix your fence so your cattle could run onto a neighbors property, you wouldn't do it because, "It wouldn't be right." It is the glue that binds people together, regardless of their differences, to live together by governing oneself in one's actions, that contribute to, rather than detract from the community.

To people living in urban America this may seem quaint and old fashioned, but remember, it is this way of living that is raising the crops and the flesh that sustain your families. It is a self governance that runs so strong throughout this part of the country that not one bank or credit union was put into receivership by the federal government in the last few years due to the foolish lending and financial gambling that went on in so many other parts of the United States. It didn't happen here because "It wouldn't be right," to run a bank or credit union like that. Too bad that wave of solid financial thinking hasn't become tsunami in size and swamped Wall Street and Washington D.C.

If you haven't noticed yet, to say I'm a revolutionary, a radical, is to understate the point. Like many Americans I think the political pot is in need of a good stirring up. Do I think fear mongering, false statements, deceit, armed aggression, and manipulation are ways to go about it? No thank you.

Also understand I am a die hard free market capitalist. For the last 30 years I've been a card carrying member of corporate America. I enjoy making money like anyone else. I've been doing so on the six major continents that all international corporations operate in, albeit on a much smaller scale. Nonetheless, I know how the game is played. That gives me the ability to spot the free market capitalists from the poseurs and frauds among us who would have us believe they support free market capitalism, but in reality do nothing of the sort.

On the subject of writing, I'm an absolute beginner, an amateur. I don't know much about it at all. So if you're selling the Brooklyn Bridge of writing or the latest penny stock that is guaranteed to make me a writing pro overnight, I may be your next sucker.

Beware though, I was raised on Royko [5], and that means not only do I understand the importance of the words, "We hold these truths to be self evident," by Thomas Jefferson of Virginia, but also, "If they don't like it, they can kiss my ass."[6], by Richard J. Daley of Chicago, in explaining American democracy in all of its colors.

One last note, those two waves mentioned at the start of all of this are big and moving, and the prevailing winds in this western edge of Montana blow east, so anyone east of here get ready. Get ready if you haven't already caught sight of those waves mentioned moving in your direction. Waves aided by the eternal winds of change. Surfs up!

[5] Royko, Mike, Pulitzer prize winning writer, and nationally syndicated columnist 1932-1997.

[6] Royko, Mike, The Chicago Daily News, What's Behind Daley's Words? February 16, 1973.

Chapter 1

"Perhaps the sentiments contained in the following pages, are not sufficiently fashionable to procure them in general favor; a long habit of not thinking a thing wrong, gives it a superficial appearance of being right." - Thomas Paine[7]

Looking across the political landscape in America today, one can see that *conservative* and *liberal* are the most overused and least understood words in our country. They are the basis for the great political scam, the great political shell game of our time. Spin the conservative-liberal shells often enough, fast enough, and the suckers....whoops, constituents....get so confused and have lost sight of where the ball might be, that they don't see the man. The man standing off to the side, pumping coins into the pockets of the operators running the shell game; party operatives, candidates, and those folks we reelect over 80 percent of the time to keep the game going. With the other hand he's grabbing billions after billions from the treasury.

This game picks up speed in even numbered years and really gets rolling every fourth of those even-numbered years. It's a big game and effective too. It will attract over 100 million Americans

---

7 Paine, Thomas, Common Sense, February 14, 1776, p.1

in those four year plays. In 2012 it attracted 127 million suckers....whoops, there goes that word again.... I mean constituents.

The aftermath, as in years past, will leave us all feeling duped. Duped again, because as before, we took our eyes off the big picture and fell for the sucker sell of the conservative-liberal shell game. The house wins again.

The house always wins, the saying goes. Well, not always if we voters understand what is really going on, what is at stake. When we do it makes it much harder for the house to stack the deck. Knowledge of what the house is up to decreases their chances of winning.

So the first thing to learn is that this whole conservative-liberal contrast in American politics is a scam, a shell game. It is the oldest political trick in the book. No matter what time in history, no matter what your polity be, whether it is a monarchy, aristocracy, theocracy, dictatorship, or even a democracy, all you need to do is to distract the royal subjects-serfs-believers-peasants-voters, get them divided and fighting amongst themselves, and their treasures, labors, and earning are yours for the taking.

This is what James Madison had in mind when trying to educate his fellow citizens, in Federalist 62, on why they should approve the new Constitution being put forth to bind the colonies together in 1788:

"Another effect of public instability is the unreasonable advantage it gives to the sagacious, the enterprising, and the moneyed few over the industrious and uniformed mass of the people. Every new regulation concerning commerce or revenue, or in any way affecting the value of the different species of property, presents a new harvest to those who watch the change, and can trace its consequences; a harvest, reared not by themselves, but by the toils and cares of the great body of their fellow-citizens. This is a state of things in which it may be said with some truth that laws are made for the *few*, not for the *many*."[8]

Madison was letting the citizens of the colonies and future Americans know through the pure propaganda of the Federalist Papers, that since times immortal, some of the wealthy and well connected have used their powers to take advantage of the masses. The ratifying of the Constitution would give the common person something they had dreamed of and died for, for thousands of years—the ability to counter balance that age old power of, "...the moneyed few." If, then and now, we stayed united in that effort to be vigilant in making sure that the laws of a nation would be made to the concerns of the *many* and not the *few*, that check on power was ours to enjoy.

The next time someone starts getting upset because they say, "...the moneyed few" are being scapegoated or unfairly singled out, and saying this is class warfare, state quietly or loudly if you prefer, "Yes, it is class warfare and it's been going on long before the Egyptians were enslaving the Israelites and Moses was screaming, 'Let my People go.'" It has been rolling right along through human history when the author of the Bill of Rights wrote the words on the preceding page, and will continue rolling along even as we try to prevent it from happening with the power of our Constitution to check that age old power the moneyed few shamelessly use to their advantage over the masses.

Repeat it over and over until it sinks in and becomes knowledge, the conservative-liberal shell game is an age old distraction scam, and the enterprising and moneyed few have been humans, being ever so human, in trying to use the masses

8 Madison, James, as Publius, The Federalist Papers, No. 62, February 27, 1788.

to their advantage since our cave days. Remember knowledge is power and knowledge doesn't happen overnight. It takes patience. It takes work. It takes time to acquire it.

Therefore it is easy to see that modern life, with its culture of instant gratification, can be a bit of a distraction. Our modern culture where you can buy now and pay later, with no money down and no interest for 18 months, where operators are standing by to confirm your pre-approved, preselected exclusive offer to the club of never-ending happiness, where universal enlightenment, organic certification, and stock market savvy can be yours. It's a place where Chinese suppliers, waiting with bated breath for a chance to manufacturer your latest must-have consumer product, are just a download away as a free App sent to you from one of your many social followers.

The buy now, pay later, no money down, and no interest until next year sales pitch that has been pumped into our brains over the airways since the 1960s has been capitalism's most persuasive slogan. We bought our cars, computers, furniture, appliances, and for some, our homes this way for over half a century. Why not our government too? Like anything, capitalism has its perversions, and this mindset may be its and the country's undoing.

Yes, why wouldn't you let all of this stand in the way of taking the time to do some in-depth political thinking? With such convenience at your fingertips, who would have the interest, let alone for 18 months, to wish to do anything more than slapping a conservative or liberal label on anyone? The same way a butcher slaps a label on a piece of meat in making your political life as simple as watching a DVD?

Let's face it, have you ever owned cotton swabs, corn, pet food, paper, a radio, a TV, a cell phone, a computer, a pager, candy, tires, planted trees, planted flowers, or had pets that were liberal or conservative? Of course you haven't because they are what they are. Humans are the same until someone slaps a label on them to codify them, to limit them, and that is exactly what the conservative and liberal labels put upon people do, limit them. Why would you want to limit someone? To control them. To get that person or people to do what you want them to do.

Therefore, it can be said that the whole conservative-liberal shell game is also a controlling mechanism put forth not to expand and encourage individual liberty, but to restrain it. This is counter to one of the basic principles of our self governing goals: maintaining and encouraging individual liberty.

As we move along in our experiment in government it is obvious that instant gratification of the consumptive part of our lives is starting to interfere with our political lives. It is now getting too much to ask people to go to a polling station and perhaps stand in line where they have to interact with other citizens to do something as simple as vote. Perhaps it's time we had a separation of consumerism and politics the way we do in church and state, so that the power of our consumeristic ways doesn't interfere with the slow deliberate process of the governing of ourselves.

The fact that people now complain because they can't vote online while those in other nations are still being tortured and killed in asking for the opportunity **to** vote shows just how spoiled we have become. Take it from someone born in the middle of the baby boom generation, never before in the history of this country have so many had so much, yet pissed, moaned, and whined about what they don't have. To anyone over the age of 80 we are a group of navel gazing spoiled brats, and we have passed on our love of instant gratification to the generations that follow us. We baby boomers even got into the wonderfully condescending habit of giving younger generations names like generation X, Y, and slackers. Even though the only difference between us and the generations that followed is the quantity of generation Xcess, we baby boomers.

 Add to this mix the ingredients of reality TV colliding with an election-year and oh boy, fasten your seat belts. Be it American Idol, Dancing with the Stars, or Creeping out with the Kartrashians, the primaries seem like any other entertainment fodder up for a possible Emmy. When a presidential candidate ends up with the Emmy for best actor in a supporting role for his or her performance on the debates, you know we will have crossed into the twilight zone, perhaps never to return to the reality we once knew.

 Returning back to the man popping coins in the pockets of the operators of the conservative-liberal shell game. Imagine for a moment the scene many of us have seen on TV and the Web of financial traders on the floors of one of the many world's exchanges. There they are waiving arms, shouting out trades to one another, while some are doing the same by computer in a quieter fashion, all doing so within the frenzied action of the floor. Brokers-dealers offer the goods: stocks, bonds, commodities, etc., and the traders bid for the contract for those goods. It is done every day, with billions and sometimes trillions changing hands.

 Now imagine the brokers being your elected representatives in Congress, and the traders are the lobbyist for special-interest. The brokers offer the goods, your tax dollars, as government contracts, and the traders bid with campaign contributions for the rights to the contract of those goods-contracts offered.

 Think it doesn't work that way? Think again. Here is the address to the Department of Defense website.[9] Take a look at where your money is going daily. If something catches your eye,

---

[9] http://www.defense.gov/Contracts/default.aspx.

look at the company getting the contract. See who they are and where the contract is being fulfilled. Now look at the senator or representative who is in that district the government contract is in. Did that elected official or their party get a contribution from said company? That's what all the lobbying, as golf outings, dinners, sporting events, etc. are about, getting their hands on our money.

It runs in the trillions of dollars, be it doctors getting reimbursed for Medicare for services rendered, or defense contractors looking to get paid for goods sold or work performed. In both cases and everywhere in between, it happens as payments for unnecessary medical procedures, or billing for military hardware costing multiples more than in the private sector. It is the private sector that is trying to scam the government (taxpayers), not the other way around.

"If men were angels no government would be necessary," but alas, as James Madison noted in Federalist 51 centuries ago, we're not. [10] That makes the hating and reviling of government our true national pastime, not baseball, seem even more ludicrous because you and I are the government. At least that was the original idea when this whole thing about our democracy started. In its purest form in America if you don't trust your government, that means you do not trust yourself or your fellow citizens, because again, you, I, and everyone else is the government.

Every time someone starts talking trash about the government, mostly Republicans these days, tell them to keep their thoughts themselves as it's getting us nowhere to constantly badmouth people, i.e. government. "Enough," you say. "I'm not the problem. It's those damn bureaucrats in government that are the problem!" You'd be partially right in that statement. More often

---

[10] Madison, James as Publius, The Federalist Papers, No. 51, February 6, 1788.

than not it is the system in which the bureaucrats work that creates the trouble of a dysfunctional and loathsome bureaucracy, not the bureaucrats/government employees themselves.

Remember none of them are promoting the conservative-liberal shell game, the way the party operatives, candidates, and incumbent officials are. Realize that before the government contract can be secured as a tax loophole, government service, or product provided, the buyer, the private sector has to make the offer. Then they include a gratuity, campaign contributions, to get the ball rolling. In today's dollars, that contribution has a 1000-to-one payoff. Every dollar that makes its way into the Democrat and Republican party coffers yields $1000 back. For the big contributors, steady year in and year out for a decade or so, the ratio jumps to roughly 3000-to-one.

A recent example is here in Montana. Arch Coal, second largest coal producer in the U.S., bid on some coal contracts in the Tongue River area of Southeast Montana in 2011. Before they bid they made a $100,000 contribution to the Democratic Governors Association when former Montana governor Brian Schweitzer, Governor B. S., the coal cowboy, was head of the Association. What did it buy them? A cool $300 million savings on the bonus bid price for the coal being offered. That is one-third of the cost of the proposed railway in the Tongue River Valley. A railway that is now owned in a three way deal between Arch Coal, billionaire Warren Buffett, and billionaire Forrest Mars. The Democratically controlled State Land Board left $300 million on the table. Three hundred million dollars that could have gone into the state treasury, yet it stayed in Arch Coal's pockets to cover their share of the cost of the railroad. All this from a $100,000 contribution, the 3000-to-one ratio.

Originally Forrest Mars of the Mars Candy fortune was in complete opposition to the railroad going through his eighty-thousand acre ranch. Once the deal was struck, and Mars became an equal partner, thereby eliminating the rails passing through his ranch, he became an ardent supporter of the railway and the coal project. Who says money can't buy you love? Another example is Microsoft. Until 1996 when Microsoft was sued by the United States Government for antitrust violations, the company never bothered to spend a nickel on lobbying or campaign contributions. Once the lawsuits started in earnest, Microsoft got religion, and got it fast. By 1998, while still being sued by the U.S. government, Microsoft made $1.5 million in political campaign contributions. The result of such action? A $1.5 billion government contract for software service in 1999. The list goes on and on, day in and day out, with your money.

This is how it works folks, so remember when we say you want your government to shrink in size, many portions of the private sector, including some of America's biggest companies, will shrink also, and with them maybe your job. That is the reality of shrinking government.

Speaking of reality, the next time someone says to you, "I am a conservative or I am a liberal," in declaring their political alliance, remember what they are also telling you, "I am an adjective; qualifier nouns, unable to stand alone, dependent," and sadly, how little they understand their own language, how foolishly they continue to allow themselves to be duped by the conservative-liberal shell game.

Conservative; adjective. Disposed to conserve existing conditions, institutions, etc. 2. cautious or moderate. 3. having the power tendency to conserve, preservative. 4. noting or pertaining to a political party whose characteristic principle is opposition to change in the institutions of the country.

Liberal; adjective: favorable to progressive or reform, as in religious or political affairs. 2. noting or pertaining to a political party advocating measures of progressive political reform. 3. favorable to or in accord with the policy of self-expression. 4. representative forms of government rather than aristocracies and monarchies. 5. giving freely or in ample measure. 6. giving freely or abundantly.[11]

Conservative or liberal, let us compare, and remember actions speak louder than words. In America today Republicans claim to be the standard bearers of conservative principles. On the periphery that seems to be the case, in particular when it comes to preserving the party's political power and wealth, but at their core that is another matter. Has it not been the Republicans in the last 30 years who sought to abolish the EPA, close down departments of Commerce and Education, reform and privatize the Postal Service, Social Security, and Amtrak? Are these not the same conservatives who want to reform Medicare and Medicaid? Are these the actions, "Noting or pertaining to a political party whose characteristic principle is opposition to change in the institutions of the country?"[12]

Then there are the Democrats, who claim to be the standard bearers of liberal principles. On the periphery that seems to be the case when it comes to progressing the party's political power and wealth, but at their core liberal is another matter. Has not been the Democrats in the last 30 years who have sought to preserve the EPA, the departments of Commerce and Education, and Amtrak? Are these not the same liberals who want to preserve the status quo in the Postal Service, Social Security, Medicare, and Medicaid? Are these the actions, "Noting or

---

[11] The American College Dictionary, Random House, © 1947-1958

[12] Ibid.

pertaining to a political party advocating measures of progressive reform?"[13]

 Yes, points can be made how each party has upheld their respective claimed political philosophies but again, what each party has displayed in their actions, over all, during the last 30 years shows quite the opposite of what they respectively claim.

 Even when it comes to spending our money, taxpayer money, both parties will devise a smokescreen of claims of how they are doing this or not doing that. Regardless of all the smoke and political distraction there is one constant during last 30 years that remains. As a good friend David Lobdell says, "When Democrats are in power they spend your money and raise taxes, and when Republicans are in power they spend your money and raise deficits."[14]

 Their mutual love of spending our money is what allies them together. A mutual dependence and support to maintain their power in the political marketplace. Not unlike the mutual alliance and dependence during the Cold War of the U.S. and Russian military. It was often said during the Cold War that the Russian and American military were in essence mutually supportive of one another thereby ensuring their own uninterrupted exertion of their influence upon their respective countries. Wary of one another to be sure, but in full understanding of their need for one another to maintain power and dominate through fear of the unknown.

Conservative or liberal government, which would you prefer?

Of all forms of government existent in the world today none is more open and free than American democracy. It is the most liberal form of government in the world. There is nothing conservative about it. That is, of course, excluding elected or

---

[13] Ibid.

[14] Lobdell, David, Petaluma, CA, August 2011.

appointed officials looking to conserve their political position or political power. Conservative government? Try the Pashto region of the Afghan-Pakistan border. Try Saudi Arabia. Try North Korea. Try anywhere but here.

If you live in the land of the free and the home of the brave and adhere to the principles laid out in the Declaration of Independence and the Constitution, politically who are you? Being the most liberal form of government by nature means the least efficient form of government. Least efficient because everyone must be heard, everyone is guaranteed a say. That takes time, that takes money, and a lot of it with a population over 300 million people. So our form of governing by default is the most expensive form of governing around. No, efficiency is not our government's middle name. That is not to say it cannot be more so, it just means it requires a different mindset, a different approach, something that will be discussed further in Chapter Four.

Here we are living in a country with the most liberal form of government in the world which most of us adhere too, so politically again who are you? Conservative, liberal, none of the above, all the above, all the above and more? If you don't fit into the stereotype cast upon you by the two major parties, why do you allow them to put you in a political straitjacket? Forced on you for the sole purpose of the parties maintaining their power and survival. There is a lot more than just conservative or liberal, Democrat or Republican, resonating, percolating throughout all of us with our political views on the country and our culture. Yet the two major parties, again aided by established media, insist we stay the course, their course, in the discussion of politics. This is how over time, they have and are squeezing the life out of the political marketplace. The harder they squeeze, the more voters opt out of calling themselves Democrats or Republicans.

As before, Independent is the third term used most today by those who have had enough of the two-party stranglehold. These people, this author included, want more say, more choice of viable legitimate candidates than what the two parties dictate we should choose. The parties effectively eliminate there being something other than right or left, conservative or liberal, Democrat or Republican, by adhering to the two-party dogma.

Independents want to vote for the person not the party, but again, through acts of legislation on the state and federal level, the ability to qualify for public office as an Independent candidate is slim to none. Who created these laws? Democrats and Republicans working together. Independents would like as many choices on the ballot as we do on a menu.

When you go to buy a car how many different choices do you have? Buying a TV, cell phone, computer, chain saw, cereal, jeans, hats, shoes, jewelry, you name it, the choices are varied and many. Imagine walking down the cereal aisle at the grocery store and seeing only two choices compared what you see today. Instead of all those choices, you'd get only two because elected officials mandated such through legislation. You'd be screaming, what happened to my freedom of choice? You'd be calling for those elected officials heads for taking away your right to choose. Wouldn't you like to have the same variety, equally displayed, in choosing a candidate for elected office as you have for anything else in life? If you're intelligent enough to choose among so many options from the food you eat to the car you drive, then you are intelligent enough to be able to handle as many choices in hiring someone to work for you, to represent you, in government. The two major parties say it's too much to ask the voters to do so. What they really mean is we don't like, and we don't want competition. So much for liberty and equality in the political marketplace.

Perhaps the finest comment I have ever heard about our presidential elections was over 20 years ago, by a then new acquaintance from Switzerland. Dieter Neuenschwander came to the United States to study English in 1991. One day in his very broken English he said, "John I don't understand your country. I go to the grocery store and I go to the mustard shelf, and I count over 26 types of mustard, twenty-six," he exclaimed excitedly, "but you only have two choices for president. In my country," he continued, "we have maybe nine or 10 kinds of mustard, but we have over 15 choices for president," he said proudly. "Your country, it's a crazy place!" It is worth noting that the Swiss have the oldest continuous direct democracy in the world. They've been at it for over 600 years and counting. One would hope it won't take America another 365 years to have 15 viable presidential candidates in the general election.

Then again, it might.

The last time there were more than two nationally recognized candidates for the job of president was in 2000 with Pat Buchanan, George Bush, Al Gore, and Ralph Nader being the four major candidates for president. A strange thing happened on the way to the election. That thing, the Commission on Presidential Debates, the CPD, is the partisan group that took over managing the presidential debates in 1987 from the nonpartisan League of Women Voters. Frank Fahrenkopf, Chairman of the Republican National Committee, and Paul Kirks, the Chairman of the Democratic National Committee, were the leaders of the newly formed CPD. They help fix the presidential marketplace in the way fixers do.

In 2000, helping the CPD on the Democratic side were Vernon-Hey Monica I got a straight up job for you at the White House-Jordan, and his Republican sidekick, James-Fuck the Jews, they don't vote for us anyway-Baker III. In that year Nader and

Buchanan were surpassing the percentage threshold set by the commission from the previous presidential election to qualify to participate in the debates. What did the commission do? They arbitrarily raised the qualifying percentage to 15 percent, effectively blocking both Buchanan and Nader in participating in the three presidential debates.

In case you forgot, Nader was given a ticket to attend the first debate in Boston in October 2000 by a supporter, but he was stopped by a Commission security consultant and Massachusetts State police. He was forced to leave under the threat of arrest for doing what any other citizen was allowed to do, go inside and watch the debate in person.[15]

This after a 15 year history highlighted on the *fair.org* website by some gems by both parties to stave off and stop competition.[16] In 1987, "Mr. Fahrenkopf indicated that the new commission on presidential debates was not likely to look with favor on including third-party candidates in the debate."[17]

"Mr. Kirk was less equivocal saying he personally believes that the panel should exclude third-party candidates from the states." "As party Chairman," says Kirk, "it's my responsibility to strengthen the two-party system."[18]

Chairman Fahrenkopf, Chairman Kirk, and Chairman Mao, three people big on rigged political systems. Chairman Murdoch is big on them too. What else would you expect from a second generation hack, hacking into phones?

Then in 1988, "The League of Women Voters is withdrawing sponsorship for the presidential debates because the demands of

---

[15] Green Party of The United States, http://www.gp.org/press/pr_04_16_02.html, April 16, 2002

[16] Fair & Accuracy In Reporting, http://www.fair.org/articles/compromised-commission.html

[17] Ibid.

[18] Ibid.

the two campaign organizations would perpetuate a fraud on the American voter."[19]

 After the Clinton and Bush campaign negotiated a behind-the-scenes deal that included the participation of Ross Perot, the CPD then invited Perot to the debates. At the time of the invitation, his standing in the four major polls averaged between seven and nine percent. The three debates are watched by a record breaking 90 million viewers.[20]

 By 1996, Perot is excluded in a two party deal sanctioned by the CPD, according to George Stephanopolous.[21] Chris Matthews questioned him at a panel discussion of the 1996 election, held at Harvard in February 1997.

"Why didn't you have the debates when people were watching?" asked Matthews, "Because we didn't want them to pay attention," Stephanopolous responded, "And the debates were a metaphor for the campaign. We wanted the debates to be a nonevent."[22]

 Both parties wanted the same in the 2000 Presidential election. Two political royal families wanted their respected brands, Bush and Gore, to be unfettered in allowing their chosen princes to debate without having to debase themselves in having commoners like Buchanan and Nader sully their royal decrees during the debates.

 Our former watchdog media, now turned lapdogs, are more than happy to follow the whims of the political royal class in constraining and helping block meaningful discussion for competition in the presidential political marketplace. They tell us

---

[19] Ibid.

[20] Ibid.

[21] Former Clinton advisor, now celebrity addled media darling. Another glaring example of the political class-media incest.

[22] Fair & Accuracy In Reporting, http://www.fair.org/articles/compromised-commission.html.

their decision to help eliminate competition in the debates is separate from the hundreds of millions of dollars they take in from advertising by the two major parties during the election. It is the media's pursuit of truth, justice, and the American way that drives them, not money, they say. "Believe us," say the media, "why would we lie to you?"

"Every person who shall monopolize or attempt to monopolize or combine or conspire with any other person or persons, to monopolize any part of the trade or commerce among the several states, or with, foreign nations, shall be deemed guilty of a felony." - Section 2, Sherman Antitrust Act.[23]

Who in America today can deny that running for the presidency, regardless of party affiliation, is a business, is commerce, and a pricey one at that? Hundreds of millions of dollars, changing hands across state lines, employing thousands of people across every state, and in many acts of commerce to help a person get elected to the White House, is a business, is interstate commerce. If that is not commerce, corporations are not of personhood.

When a group of people, the Commission for Presidential Debates, get together and arbitrarily set standards for who may or may not participate in said debates, and doing so knowing the standards they set can only be achieved by the two major parties which the commission represents, they are conspiring to monopolize the commerce of the Presidential Candidates market.

What, in reality, are presidential candidates? Salespeople peddling or promoting the product of the large organization in the hopes of convincing the majority that their product, political ideals, is the better mouse trap. What are the rewards for winning the contract for supplying this supposedly better

[23] The Sherman Antitrust Act, July 2, 1890, Ch. 647, 26 Stat. 209, 15 U.S.C. 1–7.

mousetrap? Access to and control over the treasury, the people's money, to be doled out to support all means of commerce by those who helped them win. Speaking of contracts, years later, the 1994 Republican Contract with America can be seen for what it truly was, the Republican Con Act with America.

In the early twentieth century the federal government, the people, saw fit to use the Sherman Antitrust Act against John D. Rockefeller in breaking up Standard Oil. In the late twentieth century the federal government saw fit to use the Act against William H. Gates III in breaking up the Microsoft monopoly. In the twenty-first century isn't it about time we saw fit to use the act against the Republican and Democratic parties in breaking up their political monopoly and open up the political marketplace to some real competition?

Did you realize that north of the border, in the 2008 Canadian general election, five Canadian political party candidates took part in the debate for the highest office in the land? The Conservatives, Liberals, Greens, New Democrats, and Bloc Quebecios were all represented.[24] Voters were not overwhelmed. Voters were not confused. The tanks didn't role, the country is still functioning just fine.

We now have a President who says he is for the support of all Americans, particularly minorities and women, to help elevate them in their struggle for equality. Did you truly think this President would show his support for the minority party presidential candidates by inviting them to participate in the presidential debates, and help elevate them in their struggle for political equality? So much for supporting the political minorities.

With such a liberal form of government you'd think our approach to who participates in the presidential debates would

---

[24] The Economist, The Americas, Please have the decency to panic, October 11, 2008, p. 51.

be the same. The CPD makes sure that doesn't happen by doing everything they can to preserve and maintain the status quo of the two-party system. Competition in the political marketplace is something we need more of today. The many choices mentioned earlier are a response to our open economic system, free market capitalism, or so it is called.

 Free market capitalism practiced in its purest form is the most liberal economic system in the world today. There is nothing conservative about it. When you hear someone say that they are a conservative business person, realize the only thing they're conservative about is conserving their wealth and economic power, everything else be damned.

 You want a conservative economic system? Try Richard Nixon's price controls of the early 1970s. The U.S. Government stepped in to control inflation and instituted price freezes on everything. It failed miserably. When the controls were lifted, prices took off, negating its temporary effect of dampening inflation. Conservative economic systems have been run by people with names like Castro, Khrushchev, and Qaddafi.   An economic system where one person and his underlings set prices and control all the shots in all things of major economic importance over people they rule.

 Further still, look at religion in this country. Conservative religion? Where? I dare you to open a phone book, if you still have one, and look in the yellow pages under churches. What do you see? Multitudes of ways to worship and praise the Almighty. If you are a Christian there's at least two dozen different churches to attend. No other country in the world is so liberal in the ability to pursue your religious beliefs. Tell me now, what is conservative in that? Imagine trying to be Jewish in Afghanistan, or Christian in Somalia. The economy, God, and government, three elements that permeate the lives of most all of us, and in America; liberal, liberal, and liberal. When you participate in all three, as most people in America do, you are being shaped and shaping three very powerful liberal forces that makes us what we are; a liberal democracy, with a liberal economy, and the most liberal pursuit of religious freedom in the world.

Notice it's not The Statue of Conservity gracing New York Harbor, it's Liberty, as in liberal, from the Latin Liber, (Freedom) v. conservative from the Latin Contra, (Against). So when you hear people, pundits, elected officials, or those running for office calling themselves conservatives and complaining about liberals and liberalism, these are people who are (contra) against (liber) freedom. What kind of American is that, someone who is against freedom? Who are all these people running for office, claiming conservative this and conservative that? *Con-servative*, are we being conned?

The term left and right in American political discourse, in case you didn't know, is a very French political invention, born of the French Revolution. Oui! Everybody talking left and right in politics are French (socialists) at heart. When all you socialists go to vote or discuss politics don't forget to thank those cheese eating surrender monkeys for helping shape our collective political state of mind. Ooo La La!

On the personal front it's every bit of a shell game that is practiced by the major parties. Our culture is awash with celebrities. Name the category and we have them. Sports, entertainment, media, politics, medicine, the list is endless. For better or for worse many of the celebrities feel it their duty to inform us of their personal political philosophies and politically, the way things ought to be. No one is larger on the American political landscape in this capacity than Rush Limbaugh, self-proclaimed voice of conservative America. He claims to be a conservative and a defender of conservative principles throughout our fair land. All well and fine, but watch what he does compared to what he says.

If like Rush, you should happen to get addicted to drugs-painkillers in Rush's case-do you get there by consuming a conservative or moderate amount, or a liberal amount? Ever hear of someone getting hooked on heroin by shooting too little?

When it was reported Rush allegedly purchased thousands of pain pills, including Hydrocodone™, OxyContin™, Xanax™, and time-release morphine in a span of six months, between March 2003 and September 2003, through multiple doctors in Florida and California, would you call that a conservative or liberal purchase of painkillers in a six month period?[25]

We now take a break from our program to have a word from our sponsor.

"Back pain got you down?"

"Unable to perform your radio talk show like you'd like to be able to?"

"Don't worry relief is here!"

"That's right, America's number one pain remedy, Oxy Conservative is here to save the day."

"Oxy-Conservative, taken liberally, will ensure the pain relief and the addiction you've always craved."

"Remember all drugs do have side effects, like severe hearing loss. In case of side effects, do not call your doctor, call your migrant house worker to obtain more."

Now back to our program.

If like Rush, or was it Lush, you have a weight problem, (in Lush's case, too much), do you get there by consuming a conservative, moderate amount of food, or a liberal, in ample measure, amount of food to get there? Ever seen an overweight

---

[25] Cote, John, South Sentinel Sun, December 13, 2005, Sec. B page 3.

Darfur refugee? If like Lush, you make nearly $50 million a year income, is that a conservative or liberal income compared to the average American?

We know what he says, but look what he does. Is he in the broadcasting business or the fraudcasting business? Is he America's number one radio broadcaster or America's number one fraudcaster? Is it Excellence in Broadcasting™ or Excellence in Fraudcasting?

Supposedly on the other side of the spectrum is former U.S. Senator and Vice President Al Gore. He's so liberal, Hollywood gave him an Oscar. Father Al, as Bone-Oh! from the Irish band Me Too refers to him, is the ordained leader of the über liberal cause, global warming. That moral crusade to rid the world of its industrial wrongs. Like any moral crusade, moral rectitude is being used liberally. Other than that there is not much liberal about it. Try getting Father Al into an open public debate on the subject. Forget it. His sermons on the subject are just that, tightly scripted and controlled so no dissenting opinion to his word is allowed. Is this what you would call a broad-minded, liberal thinking approach?

Is Father Al's alluding to global warming skeptics as racist stretching the cultural rubber band past its breaking point? Is using 1960s Alabama segregationist Bull Connor and his Klan as examples of the mindset of those who don't cotton to Father Al's point of view a progressive, open-minded approach to discussing global warming? Are not such tactics taking the discussion off the table of intelligent thinking and putting it into the fire of overheated rhetoric, fueled by the abundant supply of moral rectitude? How about one of Al's followers, Ellen Goodman, syndicated columnist for The Boston Globe " ...let's just say that global warming deniers are now on a par with Holocaust deniers, though one denies the past, the other denies the present and the future."[26] Hardly what one would call being tolerant to the ideas of others, a cornerstone of liberal political thinking and policy.

Returning to the Hollywood connection on this subject, Hollywood is big in supporting this cause. Partly to massage themselves and the public into believing that by driving hybrid autos and wearing natural fiber clothes all is normal for the participants in the land of make believe. Even 'true' stories get embellished in special effects proportions in La-La Land, so any cause these folks are behind is suspect in just how real it truly is.

My objection to global warming comes not from the idea itself or a rejection of the idea of living a less consuming and polluting life, but from the idea that a computer model, technology, has a greater say in all of this than I. That somehow technology knows more about what is going on outside than my own senses do. I am told that I must believe that a computer is better than I at interpreting the arching April squalls outside my windows right now as they spill their guts in a tearful display after surviving the pain of crashing into another mountain range.

On they go, doing it repeatedly until they have exhausted their tears and evaporate into thin air on the edge of the Lewis Over-thrust [27], only to be reborn as Joni Mitchell's ice cream castles in the air above the vast ocean of the Great Plains

Forgive me, it is not the change of climate I have doubts about, but the technology which has seduced many into thinking it can do no wrong, that it can give no false information. The same kind of technology used by the world's best and brightest in mathematics with their algorithms to punch holes in the world

---

[26] Goodman, Ellen, The Boston Globe February 9, 2007, A. 19 Op-ed.

[27] Eastern edge of the Rocky Mountains in Northern Montana into Canada.

financial system with their CDOs and SIVs.[28] The same way we punch holes in our hearts when we forsake who we are, for the title or position we've become. To say I have doubts about the abilities of this technology is to acknowledge the programmer's inability to program every aspect of life, including the soul, to come up with a concise answer to a defined path that the climate will take today or anytime in the future.

Norman Mailer made this clear in 2002, "That the purpose of human beings on earth is not to obtain more and more technological power, but to refine their souls. This is the deep divide that now goes on even with many Americans: What does it profit me if I gain the entire world and lose my soul."[29]

Few in humanity have ever been able to accurately predict the future. In the world I have and do inhabit, H.G. Wells, a science fiction writer, and Native American medicine men have been able to see the future with better clarity than universities full of Doctorates with their computers.[30]

If you're so concerned about the change in climate, then drop the technology you hold so dear and go outside in the climate. Revel in it, cry in it, laughing in it, love in it, do it every day, and the climate and its changes will be less and less fear-filling and less annoying because you'll understand it better. When you step outside you may come to understand that as the wind blows through your hair you feel the same thing the Earth does when the wind blows through the grasses and trees. While you're watching the branches of the trees soar and descend with the pulse of the wind, the same way birds do as they spread their

[28] Collateralized Debt Obligations and Structured Investment Vehicles. Key elements of the recent financial crisis.

[29] Rader, Dotson, *The Sunday Times Magazine*, The Times of London, Speaking Out: an interview with Norman Mailer, September 8, 2002, page 44.

[30] H.G Wells predicted; nuclear weapons, moon landing, genetic engineering, lasers, and World War II.

wings and fly, it will be easy to comprehend why the Haida [31] word for feather and leaf is the same. Who knows, someday you may be standing outside and as you look up to see the random assortment of clouds passing overhead through the sky, you may come to realize they are no different from the random assortment of thoughts passing through your head on any given day.

What aspect of technology that you use or have faith in can give you that feeling you feel when you discover something you never knew or felt before, or when you allow your humanity, not technology, to do your, 'modeling,' for you? Heartless machines producing soulless conclusions, presented to us by individuals with hearts and souls full of passion to save the planet is a bit of an ironic affair is it not? So I remain a skeptic, and not of the change in climate itself, but of the technology that produces the conclusions I am told are absolute.

Global warming is another issue picked up by those in the political establishment to be used as another shell game, them versus us, to keep the populace distracted and divided while their paymasters keep pilfering our cash. Recall Father Al Gore's visit to Glacier National Park in 1996. He walked out on to the receding Grinnell Glacier and declared it was proof global warming was real. He also declared in 1996 that he was running for Vice President again. That year he was also doing what all professional politicians do, looking for a popular issue to support so he could hopefully gain more votes in the upcoming election. An Inconvenient Truth indeed. Yes, the man who claimed to have invented the Internet, who claimed his marriage was the basis for the movie, 'Love Story,' and was raised by his father to become President of the United States, has never stopped being a politician.

---

[31] Native North American tribes indigenous to the Pacific coast of British Columbia, Canada.

You can listen to Al and Rush, and everyone in between all day long and all they will talk is conservative or liberal, Democrat or Republican, them against us, us against them, divide and conquer, but never a word about united, as in the United States. Never about what we can do together. Why? They don't care about anything other than promoting themselves. Otherwise they, too, would be talking about all the voters who no longer care to call themselves Democrats or Republicans, left or right, liberal or conservative.

Another wonderful misconception over the last several decades in America is the one we hear regularly, "The private sector can do things far better and with less waste than the government." This has been a steady drumbeat of most of Corporate America. Their constant complaint is government interference and ineptitude prevents them from being more profitable, more efficient. Translation: we want to be able dictate even more than we do now, and we all want the, 'indefinite-delivery-indefinite-quantity contracts.'[32]

The push to privatize many entities the government now runs has been a foundation block of Republican ideals for years. Let free market capitalism loose on the overburdening and wasteful government agencies, say the Republicans, and the country will be better off. Translation: we want more control of the federal budget than we have now, so we can give away even more your tax dollars to our biggest contributors than we can presently get away with.

Free market capitalism's basic premise is the shameless exploitation of inefficiencies in the market for profit or gain. Without those inefficiencies capitalism would collapse on itself. This is the reason, within America, that the private sector has become so profitable when dealing directly with the

---

[32] The most sought after of Government contracts. It is a blank check contract.

government. The inefficiency abounds to be exploited. Inefficiency that has the Pentagon paying a ridiculous sum for a dime-sized roller assembly that cost the manufacturer, Boeing, pennies on the dollar. Remember again, it is the private sector doing the exploiting of the government not the other way around. This brings us to that wonderful modern Republican political candidate declaration, we need to run the government more like a business.

This statement is worth serious consideration on two points, tragedy and comedy. The tragedy being, should government become more efficient in its operation, much of the private sector, like Boeing, would falter greatly due to the lack of inefficiency to be exploited, profited from, in dealing with the government. Goodbye socialized profitability, hello shrunken revenues. With it, shrunken employment roles for the company.

The other point, comedy, is where the fun begins. Okay, so we should run government more like a business. Which business should government be more like in its operation, Enron, WorldCom, Bear Stearns, Lehman Brothers, AIG, General Motors, Chrysler, Citibank, Goldman Sachs, Merrill Lynch, JP Morgan Chase, or General Electric? Which of these fine companies, which were run so poorly by such overpaid inept fools that they ran their respective companies into the ground and into the taxpayers pockets, should big bad government emulate?

It was the CEOs of the majority the companies just mentioned who persuaded the government not to regulate financial derivatives, the true core of the financial meltdown. These are the highly unstable, man-made atoms central to the atomic structure of modern-day financial instruments. Like any man made atom, highly volatile and very, very dangerous if misused.

Why else would Warren Buffett have called them financial weapons of mass destruction?[33]

In over 220 years of U.S. government operation the United States government still has not been able, through its alleged overwhelming incompetence, to bring the world economy to its knees. The private sector did it in less than 80 years. Now that's efficiency any MBA graduate can be proud of. Okay, so I concede the point the private sector can do things more efficiently than government. I just didn't think trashing the world economy was tops on anyone's list.

When the legendary Peter Drucker, whom the Wall Street Journal called, "the first philosopher of management,"[34] died in November of 2005, the Journal paid tribute to the man in an Op-ed piece titled, "An American Sage." In it were shining nuggets from his philosophy on management, including, "Is Executive Pay Excessive?" May 23, 1977.[35]

"Economically, [the] few very large executive salaries are quite unimportant. Socially, they do enormous damage. They are highly visible and highly publicized. And they are therefore taken as typical, rather than the extreme exceptions that they are. If and when the attack on the "excessive compensation of executives" is launched- and I very much fear that it will come soon-business will complain about the public's "economic illiteracy" and will bemoan the public's "hostility to business." But business will only have itself to blame. It is a business responsibility, but also a business self interest, to develop a sensible executive compensation structure that portrays economic reality and asserts and codifies the achievement of U.S.

33 Buffett, Warren, http://news.bbc.co.uk/2/hi/2817995.stm, BBC. March 4, 2003.

34 *Wall Street Journal*, An American Sage, November 14, 2005, p. A 22.

35 Ibid.

business in this century: the steady narrowing of the income gap between the "boss man" and the "working man."[36]

 Do you think Jamie Dimon, Jeff Immelt, John Thain, and all the other overpaid poseurs ever paid attention? Thirty-five years ago it was laid out for them as plain as the noses on their faces about the way to manage a business that would do well to compensate them and enrich the workers of this country as well, but did they heed such practical thinking? Are they tired of the,"Soak the Rich," declarations? Tired of Occupy Wall Street? Look in the mirror little boys and you'll see the subversives and the instigators of it all. Be thankful, be very thankful, and ever grateful that when you came to us, the taxpayer, in 2008 looking for a handout to pay off your gambling debts that we didn't put you into receivership, strip you from your position, and use the Racketeer Influenced and Corrupt Organizations Act to seize your questionable, illegitimately gotten gains.

 If we have learned anything from the latest financial boondoggle it is this: the private sector can be as corrupt, inept, loathsome, foolish, and wasteful as any accusations leveled against any government organization, institution, or employee in the history of this nation.

 The endless complaints that we are over-regulated, and that *removing* regulation is the elixir to all our problems is as empty headed as empty headed can be. Why do we have so many regulations? Because we have so many people and organizations that either refuse or evade following the rule of the law. New regulations are passed each time someone or some group fails to comply. It's the result of human beings being oh-so-human in wanting to not follow the rules everyone else is expected to.

 You cannot drink alcohol and drive, that's the law. It's simple enough, don't do it. Yet look at the legislative gymnastics created

---

[36] Ibid.

in every state because of those who flaunt the law. Yes, many of
the laws are absurd. Why? They are in response to people who
are even more absurd in not wanting to accept responsibility for
their actions. People unwilling to use any self-discipline, any
self-governing. Something we have seen all too much of in the
actions of those in positions of financial, industrial, military, and
political power. The 'victim' society that in many ways is
growing in size, in this and other countries, is, in part, a result of
no one at the top being willing to own up to their mistakes, and
therefore setting a bad example for all to follow.

There are plenty of good examples to follow, but mostly we
forget, or never paid attention to begin with, because our
modern media had a product to peddle which, in their revenue
hungry minds, far outshone anything else. One good example
presented to us was done by a foreign head of state when the
country of his birth became newly democratic in 1990.

When Vaclav Havel the poet and playwright turned president of
the new democratic Czech Republic addressed the U.S. Congress
in February 1990 he spoke in terms which many, including the
U.S. House historian at the time, claimed to be the finest speech
ever given by a foreign head of state in the history of the United
States Congress. His speech is as pertinent today as it was over
20 years ago in the message it relates to all those who seek
democracy, and those who wish to understand their own
democracy better.

"As long as people are people, democracy in the full sense of the
word will always be no more than an ideal; one may approach it
as one would a horizon, in ways that may be better or worse, but
it can never be fully attained. In this sense you [U.S.] are merely
approaching democracy. You have thousands of problems of all
kinds, as other countries do. But you have one great advantage:
you have been approaching democracy uninterrupted for more

than 200 years, and your journey towards the horizon has never been interrupted by a totalitarian system."[37]

This is something we should never forget, that our democracy is not just a form of government, but a journey. Another step in the journey of humanity to seek a freer way of governing ourselves, our lives. A journey humans have been on for thousands of years, in and through all the various forms of governing that have brought us to where we are today. This is an important point when considering another misconception in America by those who would espouse the family values mantra. Values, the proponents of which, would have us believe are superior to the path, the direction, the country is now traveling on, towards the horizon former President Havel mentioned.

This idea of mom, dad, and 2.2 children living in a traditional marriage, living a pious life, is sold as the only way to stabilize and improve the path of America's future. This is to say the only way we can get to the reality of what is to be, is by living in the fantasy of what used to be. The fantasy of a 1950s Hollywood TV family.

It's a great fantasy, a sales pitch, but that's all it is. With it the family values crowd wants us to stop, turn around, walk back to the past, and away from approaching that distant horizon. The other problem with this fantasy is that it gets run over by reality. The reality of American family life brought to us courtesy of our current President. A reality that acts like an IED [38] on the fantasy's progress. A biracial man born of a Caucasian mother and a Kenyan father, raised by his mother and his maternal grandparents to achieve the highest political office in the land, shreds the family values fantasy with the shrapnel of modern American cultural reality.

---

[37] Czech President Vaclav Havel, Joint session of Congress, February 21, 1990.

[38] Improvised Explosive Device, aka, home made bomb.

That's right single mothers of America, your children can now be recognized as having the potential and possibility of achieving the same. Try that trick in any other country in the world. Yes, it will happen elsewhere, but again the United States blazed a new trail in democracy.

That this is happening in America should shock no one who grew up here or lives here. After all, our current President's predecessor in the White House was a self-admitted former drug addict. A former drug addict, an alcoholic, who admitted committing a crime while under the influence of his addiction. So yes former drug addicts and children of single mothers, you too can attain the presidency.

What's next?

Sooner than most Americans realize, and to the horror of the family values crowd, we are but a generation or two away from the day when a person raised by two dads or two moms achieves the same. When state after state accept same-sex marriages as legal, and those numbers grow to be the majority of the states, the above will happen. The consequences for gay Americans will be two-sided, as all swords that cut through cultural and social stigmas are.

On the one side will be the achievement of real political equality, giving greater security and political foundation to those whose partner preference is of their own sex. Once secure, the other side of the blade will show itself. Those future generations of gays who will define their sexual preference by definition of choice, accident, and yes, divine intervention. No longer bound to the cultural dogma of one idea of why a person is gay, born that way, future generations of gays will be at liberty to take that singular idea and run with it. Run with it the way we Americans do with anything cultural, political, or religious. That is, stretch it, pull it, and expand it in every direction, like a piece of Silly Putty™.

When that time appears, statements like those from actor Cynthia Nixon, "I say it doesn't matter if we flew here or we swam here, it matters that we are here and we are one group and let us stop trying to make a litmus test for who is considered gay and who is not,"[39] won't raise an eyebrow, least of all in the gay community.

This is the natural course of things be it cultural, political, or religious. In their beginnings all of these require a foundation, i.e. beliefs, which the followers and believers can adhere to. The beliefs, the dogma, are there to build the following, maintain existence, and ultimately achieve acceptance throughout society as a whole. These beliefs are of particular importance during the building and maintaining stages of the process. Collectively they are the glue that binds and the shield that protects the adherents of those beliefs until the battle for acceptance has been won. Once acceptance has been realized throughout society as a whole, the dogma becomes less of a protective shield because the constant need to defend the dogma lessens over time. At some point the expansion of the dogma, and in some cases what some would call the corruption or perversion of the dogma, starts to take on a life of its own. What cultural, political, or religious beliefs over time haven't followed this pattern? Present-day gay dogma, over time, will do the same, and in doing so lay waste to the ideas of the family values crowd.

The last misconception addressed in this chapter is one of the greatest in modern America. The idea that you can lower taxes, shrink government, and expand the military all at the same time. It is worse than a misconception, it is another classic shell game.

---

[39] Witchel, Alex, The New York Times Magazine, *The New York Times*, Jan.22 , 2012, p.27.

Put upon America mainly by Republicans with backstop support from Democrats. It was originally used by Republicans as a tool to get elected.

Over the last 30 years it has morphed into an accepted truth that has now come back to haunt Republicans as the Tea Party. These are the people who believe the idea to be the real way the government functions, rather than the political sales pitch it truthfully is. Telling Tea Party members it isn't real is like telling a child for the first time that Santa Claus isn't real. The reaction, like a child's, covers the spectrum. The disappointment and the delusion members the Tea Party now feel caused by the realization that they have been conned only to get their votes is no less the disappointment and delusion America's young voters feel who came to the realization that they too had been conned only to have it done to them by our current President and the Democrats to get their votes.

This would explain why the new Tea Party Republicans in the House of Representatives balked at the idea of raising the national debt within nine months of being sworn into office in 2011. When House Speaker Boehner told them to, "Get in line," in voting for the increase, he became in the eyes of the new Tea Party members of Congress, the Grinch that stole the Less Taxes, Smaller Government Christmas.

Five thousand years of human political history shows repeatedly that as armies are formed and increase in size, no matter what form of government has existed, taxes increase, and the bureaucracy expands. Yet the word from Washington D.C. over the last 30 years is one of lowering taxes, shrinking government, and maintaining the largest military on the globe. Thirty years of that lie has come home to roost as burgeoning national debt. A debt brought on in no small way and directly related to the unwillingness of Democrats and Republicans to be honest with the electorate of the true costs, year after year, in maintaining such a large military force throughout the world.

It all started with such great fanfare under the spell of the Great Communicator, President Ronald Reagan. He sold this falsehood, this lie, the same way he sold soap on the GE Theater in the early 1960s. By the time he got done selling, the national debt went from $997 billion to $2.85 trillion.[40] This was after roughly 12 different tax increases in eight years caused by the massive military spending to bankrupt the Soviet Union.

This continued military buildup is why the Great Read My Lips, President George H. Bush, recanted his no new taxes pledge. He had to. He had no choice as the cost of his last military escapade, *The Mother of All Battles*, proved so costly the annual deficit was $300 billion and growing. Even with his no new taxes retreat, the debt advanced to $4.4 trillion, jumping over 50 percent in 4 years.[41]

By the time the Great Philanderer, President Bill Clinton, left office and the end of the Cold War was a distant memory, the debt climbed to $5.8 trillion, roughly a 25 percent increase.[42] The dollar amount was less in eight years than those of the Great Read My Lips in four years. Why? We reduced our military for the first time in decades. The Great Philanderer wanted, but didn't get all the military reductions he asked for. Democrats and Republicans in Congress from our states did everything they could to block the President's military base closure plans, making sure on the local level, where it was most visible, the lie continued to live and grow. The loss of military expenditures were some other state's problem, and let it be that way. The local

---

[40] http://www.treasurydirect.gov/govt/reports/pd/histdebt/histdebt.htm. 9/30/81-9/30/89.

[41] Ibid.

[42] Ibid.

military base stayed open for business on dollars that were borrowed, so why should we care?

Then in 2001 the Great Decider, President George W. Bush, and his posse, including ace sharpshooter Deferment Dick rode into the Beltway. By the time the Great Decider and Vice President Deficits Don't Matter Dick Cheney were through with the country the national debt doubled to just shy of $12 trillion.[43] All for the glory of a son to prove to his father he was a real man. All for the glory of the second-in-command to prove he was tough enough, man enough. Put another way, the $6.1 trillion added to the national debt for the Great Decider to prove his manhood in eight years was greater in dollars than the increase in dollars from Presidents Truman through Clinton, a span of over 50 years. Then came the Great Yes We Can, President Barrack Obama, and he has let us continue to believe that, yes we can continue this idiocy. All this has caused a very simple and fundamental foundation in the forming and running of all governments to be lost on the majority of Americans: the bigger your army, the bigger your bureaucracy, the more money you need to pay for it.

Don't believe this is a fundamental of American democracy? Go ask the Republicans. The Republicans in the U.S. Congress in 1800. "On New Year's Day, 1800, the Republicans suddenly put forward a resolution to disband the army that had been created in the aftermath of the XYZ affair. The Army had proven both expensive and unpopular, and Washington, its nominal commander, was dead. With the Ellisworth mission en route to Paris and the crisis with France winding down, it made eminent sense to do away with the new army and save the country an impending $5 million deficit."[44]

43 Ibid.

44 Smith, Jean Edward, *John Marshall, Definer of a Nation*, Henry Holt,1996, p.256-257.

How about a word or two from the original Republican, Thomas Jefferson? In Jefferson's first State of the Union address he addressed the issues of cutting taxes, reducing the size of government, and—pay attention Republicans and Tea Partiers— *scaling back the military.*

Jefferson's calls for reducing the military were for both the Army and the Navy to be scaled back in size. Part of his original plan was to close many garrisons and many forts, i.e. military bases, for lack of use. They proved too expensive to maintain. The occupants of revolutionary America, whether they fought or not, were well aware of the very expensive nature of a standing army. The Continental Army that wasted away at Valley Forge did so because of lack of funds to equip and feed them through a very tough winter.

From the Great Communicator through the Great Read My Lips, the Great Philanderer, the Great Decider, and on to the Great Yes We Can, the Great Lie has rolled along, crushing all in its path, and gaining size year after year until it has taken on, in size and scale, Santa Claus proportions. A size in dollars inconceivable to the average citizen. Along the way the conservative-liberal shell game continued to intensify with every new federal budget. The shifting back and forth kept the electorate distracted. Distracted like Dorothy and her friends in front of the overwhelming illusion of the great and powerful Oz, so as not to see or, "Pay no attention to the man behind the curtain." [45]

Ironically, the Great Lie was put upon us by the Great Communicator because of the man behind the curtain, The Iron Curtain. It's where the Evil Empire lurked, ready to strike down truth, justice, and the American way! We had to spend militarily we were told. The fate of the free world called for it, demanded it. So did your elected representatives in Congress, eager to make

[45] Baum, L. Frank, *The Wonderful Wizard of Oz*, George M.Hill Company, 1900.

sure the federal dollars continued to flow into their district or state, thereby ensuring their steady employment. Steadily employed at keeping the conservative-liberal, Democrat-Republican shell game moving fast. Fast enough that most of us kept buying right into it.

It moved so fast over the last 15 years we did something we never did in our history, not raise taxes while engaged in battle on two fronts. For 30 years we have bought the Great Lie. Had it been bought with cash from our pockets we wouldn't feel like we do now, but we didn't. We bought the Great Lie with borrowed money. Now all we have is the debt.

As Walter Lippmann explained in 1926, "The fundamental reason why these great international war debts cannot be regarded as ordinary debts is because they are dead. They do not represent capital invested in a living enterprise….money borrowed to build a railroad earns money to pay for itself. But money borrowed to fight a war produces nothing, and if it has to be paid it becomes a dead mortgage superimposed upon all living credits of a nation."[46]

Dead debt giving us dead soldiers, brought on by deadbeat politicians elected by a deadbeat majority. Like the deadbeat dad syndrome on steroids. Start something, help create something, but not following through with the money, time, and love of it all to deal with it properly. Thirty years of not thinking a thing wrong, slowly, steadily gave it a superficial appearance of being right. Right into a debt to be paid long after those who fought those wars are dead and gone.

All of this happened because the people we elected and the people they have appointed as civilian military leaders couldn't plan or fight their way out of a bathroom stall if their lives depended on it. This is in stark contrast to those in the military

---

[46] Lippmann, Walter, *New York World*, July 29, 1926.

who can and do embody the best of what our military has to offer in military skills. Something British citizen Emma Sky, who worked side by side with some of America's highest military commanders in Iraq for years knows very well. Her comment about General Raymond Odierno tells us everything we need to know about soldiers like him, "I would have followed him anywhere."[47]

Add to the above the following, and it becomes clear how we got where we are fiscally today. During the start of the Great Communicator years, with the Democrat's control of Congress, the annual deficits started to rise. What to do? Congress's solution was simple. Do what they had done starting back in the Great Society years, take money intended for the Social Security Trust Fund and apply it to the general fund, thereby making the deficit look smaller than it truly was. This sleight-of-hand was the continuance of the IOUs to the Social Security Trust Fund. All of this rolled along, but by the early 1990s those in government realized they had a problem on their hands. The sleight-of-hand going on was causing problems for future payment projections for Social Security funding, Medicaid, Medicare, and the military, as the government's continued deficit spending would ensure problems for all.

Enter the Great Philanderer with Federal Reserve chief Alan Greenspan bending his ear on deficit reduction, by controlling presidential discretionary spending, which the President obliges. Next come the Republicans as they take over the Congress in 1994 and the Republican Con Act with America. A con act because, while indeed the Republicans sought to reduce the federal largess, they too decided to use the same shifting of funds racket. To help it along the Republicans and Democrats in the Republican-controlled Congress decided to form a new

47 Hopkins, Nick, The Guardian Weekly, Learning the limits of our power, July 27, 2012, p.14.

commission to investigate the Consumer Price Index, the CPI. It was known as the Boskin Commission, made up of so-called esteemed economists, and set up to find out if government was calculating annual inflation correctly. A vital thing to know with having to project out governments liabilities for the greatest chunk of future federal spending in Medicaid, Medicare, the military, and Social Security. What were the commissions findings? Oh, government got it wrong on the inflation projection because of the CPI. The Boskin Commission came to the conclusion that the CPI included two unrealistic categories to which inflation was being calculated. Those two categories? Food and fuel.

The backbone of the American, let alone the world, economy, but nonetheless trivial in the Commissioner's eyes in needing to calculate real inflation. The commission came to the conclusion they were no longer needed so they recommended Congress removed them from the CPI. This was and is a wonderful intellectual pursuit to say the least. In real life it is like saying your eyes and your ears cloud or misrepresent what you perceive as reality so you don't need them, they should be removed, and then you will perceive life correctly.

Why did the Republicans and Democrats in the Republican-controlled Congress agree to this nonsense? Because they needed to tap the inflation number way down to maintain the fantasy that everything was okay, and spending and revenues were hunky-dory. If food and fuel stayed in the CPI, the forward projections of funds needed to run the government based on the real inflation we all saw every year in the grocery store and at the gas pump would be unattainable based on the current spending and revenue patterns from 1996 on. Get rid of food and fuel in the CPI, and Congress made it appear all was going to be okay. Okay until they got out of town with their congressional pensions intact, like former Senator Alan Simpson.

Another consequence intended or not of this sleight-of-hand was the effect it had on private-sector wages. If the government could state, falsely, that real inflation was negligible year after year, who then could get a reasonable raise every year to match the rise in the cost at the pump and at the store? Taking the understated rate of inflation put out by the government year after year since the mid 1990s and it's easy to see why real wages have stagnated relative to all other price increases. Take real inflation, including food and fuel, into account, and the minimum wage would be over $12 an hour today, which means everyone else's wages would have risen also. Someone being paid $20,000 annually in income in 1996 would be making $30,000 in annual income today. Someone making $30,000 in 1996 in income would be making roughly $45,000 in income today.

With wages rising realistically with real inflation, a key component to national security and economic stability would have been realized, the rising value of a person and his or her talents. An asset far more important to the long-term health of the country, both politically and economically, than the inflated value of all the houses in America, and all the gold in China.

The backdrop to all of this was the continued efforts by the Federal Reserve to keep interest rates low, at times artificially so. They had to, to meet the demand for the increased borrowing by the government in keeping the government's interest rate costs down. A byproduct of this was to help make the rich richer still. With the long-term average of a seven percent annual return on investments being the benchmark of the stock market since the late 1800s, anything above that, on an annual basis, is considered gravy by traditional investment standards.

In the early 1990s, with interest rates having been around three percent, how difficult was it for someone with the financial means to borrow money at three percent, buy a government-backed bond paying seven percent, and long term safely doubling your money along the way. Doubling your money off a loan with three percent interest is much easier than trying to do so borrowing money at seven or eight percent, when again, the long term average is a seven percent return. Yes, keep the CPI numbers fraudulently low and you can keep interest rates artificially low too. Using borrowed money, or margin, as it is called, is how the rich kept getting richer.

Compare that to today where real interest rates are nearly zero percent. U.S. government bonds are now paying just shy of three percent, so to be able to borrow money at a half percent interest and buy government bonds paying almost three percent, that's making almost five times the return on your initial investment, long term. In days past that used to be enough, but in today's Wall Street world making the seven percent return on your investment, let alone five times your investment, is not enough. Leveraging, or on margin, now has to be 30 to 40 times to be considered a worthwhile investment. And you wonder why the nearly three trillion dollars in extra cash that corporate America is hanging onto is not being invested in capital spending to create new industries to hire you? Two words; fear and greed. As Thomas Paine noted, "The rich are in general slaves to fear."[48]

Their access to such funding being far easier for the average person, makes this all too easy for those in the upper echelons of our country to do this. Many an average income earner wanted to join the game too, but not having the increase in annual salary that the phony cost-of-living data and faux low inflation scam was precipitating, they turned to the only investment they could,

---

[48] Paine, Thomas, Common Sense, 1776, p.40.

the housing market. With all the excess money generated by falsely low interest rates, the money had to go somewhere. Some of it went into paper assets, inflating those to unreal values, think—Dot.com bust—and some of that excess spilled into real assets, like real estate.

We all know the rest of the story. We all also know much of this was dominated by the folks behind the scenes helping pull the levers to make it all happen: America's largest financial institutions and corporations which delved deeply into the financial game. A sector of society purposely devoid of women, minorities, and independent thinking. That sector of society, where, CEO is monarch and everyone below their royal court— read Board of Directors—are serfs to serve the desires of the royal few.

If something as simple as leaving the cost of fuel and food in the CPI had continued, real wages would have risen along with real values of inflation. Which means people would have made more money. Which means those people would have paid more in taxes. Which means, of course, the government would have taken in more revenue, but that increase in revenue would have been offset by the reality that real inflation would have forced Congress to sit down and deal with the expanding costs of Social Security, Medicare, Medicaid, defense spending, and dealt with them by cutting spending realistically over a 20 to 40 year period.

The Great Philanderer and Congress did do this to a certain extent, but not to that level truly necessary to bring revenues and spending in line. The claimed budget surpluses at the change of the millennium were the product of the same smoke and mirrors of the warping of the CPI. Had the CPI not been changed in the mid 1990s, it would still have shown to run an annual deficit, not an imagined surplus as we were told, because the interest payments on the debt would have risen enough with real inflation to show annual deficits.

If they had not made these changes to the CPI in figuring inflation, who or what would have suffered? Realistically, it may have cost us one to two percentage points of Gross Domestic Product (GDP) annually over the years, but the pain would have been something we could have dealt with on an annual basis because it would have been spread out over nearly two decades. Corporate profits would surely have taken a hit because of higher borrowing costs and higher labor costs, but again absorbed over a two decade span, something painful, but not debilitating. Not debilitating like today, as all the above has come home to roost, all at the same time. Yes, the economic and social pain we are experiencing today is 30 plus years rolled into the last several years.

History has caught us again. We who grew up in the rebellious 1960s and early 1970s with our, 'Down with the Man, Power to the People, Death to Corporate Power, and Stop the Military' protests and sit ins have become the Man, the Corporate Power, and the military. What do have to show for it? Perhaps a better question is: what are we giving future generations to look forward to?

Take away hope and you steal the soul of a nation. Do we leave the generations that follow nothing more than the thousand yard stare? That thousand yard stare I saw repeatedly every time I crossed the Iron Curtain into East Germany in the mid 1980s. That stare that said everything about a people who had given up, resigned to complacency, and void of the idea of optimism.

Is that the horizon we want future generations to see? A horizon they've stopped walking towards because of the curtain of financial idiocy and cynicism we've erected before them. In allowing ourselves to be distracted by the smoke and mirrors put upon us by those in political power, we took our collective eyes off the eight ball. The eight ball of practical financial planning for ourselves, and for the country. Shell games are great on New York City Street corners or riding on the "L" in Chicago, but obviously long term, a foolish way to run economic or political policy in a country.

Are you angry? You should be. Angry at those who we hired to regulate this stuff, but also angry at ourselves for foolishly rehiring the same people every two, four, or six years who promise us the sky and the moon during the campaign, but don't follow through once elected. U.S. Supreme Court Chief Justice John Roberts clarified this recently,"It is not our job to protect the people from the consequences of their political choices."[49]

Here we are America, and now what are we going do? Will we keep playing those empty shell games, those empty shell games which got us here, which will keep us where we are, or will we work our way out of this? Maybe we should start listening to those around us who said goodbye to the Democrats and Republicans and declared their independence as voters. Maybe there is a way forward from all of this that doesn't start with our yearning for the good old days. Not reaching for what used to be, rather, reaching for what we have at hand in the present. No longer, as Ben Tarnoff wrote, "What might be called Founders nostalgia, a narrative of national decline that contrasts the impoverished present with the memory of American's mythic creation."[50]

Let's start with what we have and see what develops. This is, after all, the longest continuous experiment in representative democracy. Recognizing we're all political lab rats in this

[49] Roberts, John, Chief Justice U.S. Supreme Court for the majority, June 28, 2012, 11-393, 11-398, and 11-400.

[50] Tarnoff, Ben, Lapham's Quarterly, Volume IV, Number 4, Fall 2011, page 218.

experiment doesn't make it any easier, it just clarifies what we are, and that we are all in this experiment together.

Chapter 2

I don't want to belong to any club that would have me as a member - Groucho Marx

If we wish to change the current situation, we need to kick the two-party habit. Like any 200-year-old addiction it won't be easy. It won't be easy because the Democrats and Republicans have been slowly, steadily, stacking the deck for over 200 years. The two parties are two of the two oldest continuously operating organizations in America. So by default they are the deepest in tradition and the slowest to change. This also means the two major parties are the most corrupt organizations due to habit, human nature, and time. Corrupting the political marketplace is as easy as breathing for these two. A few examples follow.

It was 1976 and the nation was celebrating the Bicentennial of the Declaration of Independence from Britain. The struggle for independence got off to a bang, literally. In Washington State they elevated the Bicentennial politically by having the largest number of minority parties in Washington State history appear on the general election ballot. Washington state citizens were expressing their political independence in an unprecedented way by putting 12 minority parties on the November ballot.

The battle for independence from the tyranny of the two-party majority system was in full force. Everyone was enjoying the right of freedom of expression in exercising their political freedoms to have so many political parties to choose from.

Well, almost everybody.

Within a year of this wonderful political expression, the Democrats and Republicans in the Washington State Legislature revised the Washington State Statute concerning elections to stop this kind of freedom dead in its tracks. Before the revision the minority parties went straight to the general election, bypassing the primary set up by the Democrats and Republicans, at tax payers expense, to choose their respective candidates. Now, with the two major parties pushing hard against the freedom of political expression, they forced minority parties into their primary and made a one percent threshold of the popular vote a requirement to move on to the general election. An unusual way to celebrate 200 years of independence from the tyranny of politically oppressive forces, don't you think? "The record demonstrates that at least part of the legislative impetus for revision of the Washington statute was concerned about minority parties having such easy access to Washington State general election ballot."[51]

Isn't it easy access to the ballot that encourages people to participate in democracy either by being listed on one or voting with one? Isn't it easy access to the ballot that had 15 different parties on the ballot the first time Iraqis were allowed to vote in 2005? From the Democratic and GOP party's reaction, by the legislative process, you would have thought the minority parties were out to destroy American democracy. All they were trying to

---

[51] White, Byron, U.S. Supreme Court Associate Justice for the majority, Ralph Munro, Secretary of State of Washington v. Socialist Workers Party, et al. No. 85-656.

do was participate in it, and now the two major parties, colluding together, were making it harder.

Another part of this revision by the Washington State legislature also changed the number of signatures required in a convention to 100, up from the previous 25, to qualify for state elected office. If you wanted to run for President of the United States or Vice President the number of signatures needed in a convention jumped to 1000 from the previous 200 participant's signatures required to be put on the general election ballot.

Notice that no restrictions were placed on any other marketplace when the selection went higher than 12. Did they declare a cereal maker or car manufacturer had to have at least one percent of the market to qualify to offer their products in those respective marketplaces? Of course not. Such actions would have been considered unethical in interfering with an open competitive marketplace. They would have been accused of trying to stymie competition. Allegations of government being heavy-handed in interfering with free enterprise would have been everywhere. Yet in the political marketplace such restraints on competition were and are accepted. In the worst of scenarios, the U.S. Supreme Court has supported this for decades.

In 1983, a special election was held in Washington State for the United States Senate seat after the death of longtime Boeing Senator Henry 'Scoop' Jackson. That special primary attracted 32 candidates, a record number for the state of Washington in the senatorial primary. One of the candidates, Mr. Peoples of the Socialist Workers Party, SWP, was on the ballot. He receive 596 of the 681,960 votes cast. He failed to make the one percent threshold to move on to the general election established by the Democrats and Republicans in Washington State legislature in 1977. Mr. Peoples and the SWP sued the state claiming their rights under the First and Fourteenth Amendments had been violated. The District Court denied the claim, but the Court of Appeals reversed it saying Washington's State law was unconstitutional. The state appealed to the U.S. Supreme Court. The lawsuit was Ralph Munro, Secretary of State of Washington v. Socialist Workers Party, et al. No. 85-656, where the court voted 7-2 in favor of the state. The earlier quote from Justice White was from the majority opinion of the court in this case.

Dissenting were Justice William J. Brennan and Justice Thurgood Marshall. Justice Marshall, knowing a thing or two about the Fourteenth Amendment, Brown v. Board of Education, and a teensy bit of knowledge about the struggles of minorities in America, wrote the dissent.

"The minority parties often unconventional positions on political debate, expand the range of issues with which the electorate are concerned, and influence the positions of the majority, in some instances becoming majority positions. And its very existence provides an outlet for voters to express their dissatisfaction with the candidate or platforms of the majority parties. Notwithstanding, the crucial role minority parties play in the American political arena, the court holds today that the associated rights of minority parties and their supporters are not unduly burdened by ballot access statute that, in practice, completely excludes minority parties from participating in statewide general elections."[52] Justice Marshall continued, "Their contribution to "diversity and competition in the marketplace of ideas," Anderson v. Celebrezze, does not inevitably implicate their ability to win elections."[53]

This concept defines our marketplace of ideas, our marketplace we all have a constitutional right to participate in, unfettered,

---

[52] Marshall, Thurgood, U.S. Supreme Court Associate Justice for the dissent, Ralph Munro, Secretary of State of Washington v. Socialist Workers Party, et al. No. 85-656.

[53] Ibid.

and unrestricted by government intervention. In the political marketplace of ideas, Democrats and Republicans continue to limit and restrict the diversity and competition Justice Marshall states we so badly need to keep our form of government vibrant and healthy.

Ideas are the oxygen of the body politic that helps nourish it and keep it alive. Starve the body politic of that oxygen and its growth is stunted, its muscles atrophy, and eventually that body withers away and dies. Much the way modern politics in America is flailing about today, gasping for new ideas, gasping for oxygen. An oxygen that is being restricted by the Democrats and Republicans in their single-minded focus to stay in power, the health of the body politic in America be damned.

Justice Marshall went further, "The only purpose this statue seems narrowly tailored to advance is the impermissible one of protecting the majority political parties from competition precisely when that competition would be most meaningful. Since Williams v. Rhodes, this Court has recognized that state legislation may not ensure the continuing supremacy of the two major parties by precluding minority party access to the ballot as a practical matter. Yet here the court sustains a statute that does just that. In doing so, the court permits the state to preempt a meaningful participation by minority parties in the political process by requiring them to demonstrate their support in a crowded primary election. The court thus holds that minor parties may be excised from the electoral process before they have fulfilled their central role in our democratic political tradition: to channel dissent into that process in a constructive fashion."[54]

If we don't channel that dissent in a constructive fashion, over time that dissent will devolve and explode in a destructive

---

[54] Ibid.

fashion. As I have stated more than once in front of legislative committee hearings, it is as simple as monkey see, monkey do. When those who've been elected, nominated, or appointed to positions of political power bend, break, or manipulate the laws as they see fit, eventually everyone else in the land will too. The question to ask then is, who are the real long-term threats to American democracy? Those pseudo Muslims, screaming Allah, that would fly a plane into a building, killing thousands, or those who work politically, quietly, and tenaciously to undermine the very foundations we stand on?

 Be it 1954 or 1986, Justice Thurgood Marshall's standards for which the nation would do well to constitutionally support its minorities, be it race or political party, remained unchanged. In 1954 the U.S. Supreme Court unanimously supported those standards. In 1986 The Court no longer did, closing a channel for constructive dissent, and thereby restricting the flow of oxygen in the body politic in America.

 This kind of foolishness just kept rolling right along and by 1998 it was getting worse. The major parties set their sights on California's open primary where everyone was on the same ballot. By the time it made it to the Supreme Court, it was 2000. In July of that year the court ruled 7-2 that the primary was unconstitutional in violating the First Amendment rights of the freedom of association of the political parties. Even though no parties existed when the Constitution was drafted.

 This rattled the folks in Washington State because the California primary was modeled after the Washington State primary. A primary that had been created 66 years earlier by the citizens of the state by way of the initiative process and put forth by the Washington State Grange, a rural agricultural organization. The law had survived several legal challenges for decades. Now the viability of the law was in question, so at the start of the 2001 legislative session in Washington State, and with the backdrop of the U.S. Supreme Court deciding the national election just a month earlier, the legislature started holding hearings on the matter.

Living in the state capital, Olympia, at the time, I made the time to express my concerns. In a hearing of the House Committee on State Government in early 2001, my testimony included the following. "We've been hearing a lot about the violation of the party's First Amendment rights of association under a blanket primary today, but what about the other constitutional issues no one is talking about? What about the right of the citizen's guarantee of due process under the Fifth and Fourteenth Amendments? How can we have a fair trial in federal court when the attorney for the defense, the people, would be aligned with the plaintiff in a possible future lawsuit against the people? Should the Democratic Party sue the people, as they are threatening to do, then the attorney will be the State's Attorney General. She is a Democrat and has been for years. Is this not a conflict of interest? Should the State's Attorney General recuse herself in being the attorney for the defense if the Democrats sue the state? Something is not right here, something no one seems to want to address."[55]

Confused looks by the committee members was the collective answer. No one would come to address this in later committee hearings held, or in private conversations with elected officials. Everyone seemed to be tone deaf, unwilling to acknowledge that surely a conflict of interest from the State's top cop might exist. Ethics were overruled by the politics of the case, by the politics of the times.

---

[55] Marshall, John, Testimony before the Washington State Legislative House Committee on State Government, January, 2001.

The question I put to the committee is a simple one that any attorney can answer. What should happen if the defense attorney is beholden or connected with the plaintiff in the case? The usual answer is, that attorney should recuse themselves from the case because they can't give the defendant proper legal representation. The defense attorney is tainted, therefore they shouldn't be there, because of a conflict of interest.

Now take that conflict of interest another step. You have a judge or judges that are to hear a case. Before the case starts, the judge or judges know the attorney for the defense is beholden, influenced by the plaintiff in the case. Does not that judge or judges have an ethical judicial obligation not to hear the case until this conflict of interest is resolved? Most sensible people would say yes. The judges have an ethical obligation, but again the politics of the times and the politics of the case overruled ethical concerns.

As it turned out the Democrats of Washington State did sue the state, later joined by the Republicans and Democratic Attorney General Christine Gregoire, by default, was attorney for the people. No one seem to be bothered by the fact that she was a card-carrying member of the plaintiff organization. No one seemed concerned that she was gunning for higher political office, as the party's choice for governor. No one seemed concerned that perhaps a deal could be cut between her and the Democratic party, in which a weak defense of the case would ensure the party's backing in a future election for governor. This last item was alleged by those involved in the case who had access to the information acknowledging such. No doubt the same thing happened in the California case too. All of these questions were brushed aside by all the courts that heard both the California case and the Washington State case.

Therefore an unintended consequence of the lawsuits brought by the major parties in the two different states against the states was to expose the Achilles' heel of the two-party system concerning open and unbiased trials of a political nature. That being, the political bias of all the players overruled the ethical and constitutional obligations of those operating in the legal system. Not allowing a lawsuit to continue until defense counsel was independent of the plaintiff in the case would be the norm.

So too, a judge setting aside a lawsuit because a defense counsel is connected to a plaintiff in a case, would happen. This happens every day in the American judicial system, but when it comes to the two major political parties looking to corrupt and stack the deck in the election process, those every day concerns evaporate under the heat of politics. How can you have due process of law with such political shenanigans going on? The same political shenanigans Chief Justice John Marshall fought so tenaciously against in his 35 years on the U.S. Supreme Court.

If this craziness makes you feel like you're living in Wackystan instead of the good old USA, wait, the wackiness has just gotten started. After unhappily losing their open primary to the hi-jinks of the major parties, the fair citizens of Washington State sought an alternative to the now forced, closed primary. Again the Washington State Grange, motivators behind original open primary, in 2004 put an initiative to the voters for a top two primary, emulating the one in Louisiana approved by the United States Supreme Court. This would allow one primary ballot with all candidates listed on it. The top two in votes, regardless of party, would move on to the general election.

The difference between this and the closed primary is like the difference between shooting yourself in your left foot versus your right foot. Either way it's going to hurt and you limp along, but the choice is yours. Oh boy! Unfortunately, the voters of

Washington State did vote in favor of it. Even though those sharp eyed gals, The League of Women Voters, tried in vain to show what a sham the top two primaries were and are.

Naturally, one of the two majors sued, the Republicans, and yes the U.S. Supreme Court took up the case, and yes they voted to support the citizens initiative. Surprised? You shouldn't be. Why wouldn't the Court support a law that would further impede the progress of Independent and Minor party candidates, as they had for Washington State in 1986 and 2004?

The League of Women Voters revealed that fact for all to see in the ballot pamphlet in their very concise argument against the initiative I–872, and their rebuttal of the argument for the initiative. It was The Court's dissenting opinion in the case that gave Wackistan Air license to fly.

Associate Justice Antonin Scalia wrote the dissent and used a gay scout master—not once but twice—and Sesame Street's Oscar the Grouch to frame the finer points of dissent as to the law's unconstitutional nature. Seems he just can't let go of the gay issue even in a case that has nothing to do with gays. You can now use Oscar the Grouch with legal arguments in your lawsuit.[56] Who's next, Bugs Bunny and Daffy Duck? This from one of the best jurists on The Court in decades. No wonder his dissent fell flat. Judicially, however brilliant he may be, as a salesman, forget it. The guy couldn't sell matches and gasoline to a pyromaniac. He couldn't sell sandbags in the middle of a 100 year flood. The product he has been hawking for years, Originalism, didn't sell well at all, so he decided to re-brand it in hopes of promoting better sales. It's now called Textualism. No matter what he calls it, it won't sell because he's a lousy salesman. So much for trying to keep politics out of the Supreme

[56] Scalia, Antonin, Associate U.S. Supreme Court Justice for the dissent, 06-713 and 06-730.

Court; again, something for which Chief Justice John Marshall worked tirelessly.

In 2007, the Republicans and Democrats in the Montana State Legislature kept up the tradition of trying to eliminate competition by rewriting election law requiring Independent candidates signature petitions for elected office to be due by early March instead of the old June deadline. Why? To make it far more difficult for Independent candidates to make it on the general election ballot. In May 2012, Federal U.S. District Judge Sam E. Haddon struck down the law as unconstitutional.[57] Steve Kelly of Bozeman, Montana sued the state with the help of two ACLU groups. Judge Haddon ruled that Montana's filing deadline for Independent candidates, "Imposes a significant barrier to the exercise of the rights protected and guaranteed by the First and Fourteenth Amendments."[58] Here again the two parties were using their political power and influence to stifle competition in the political marketplace.

It is the specter of undue political influence by the two major parties that restricted, and continues to restrict and repress participation in the political process by Independents, minorities, minority parties, and women. When I refer to the undue political influence of the two major parties, I am not referring to all the parties members actively creating this scenario, I am referring to something altogether different that was briefly mentioned earlier.

In Samuel E. Finer's, History of Government, we find the following passage commenting on the evolution of political parties during the Industrial Revolution, "But it was not until near universal suffrage had emerged that the notables lost their place in the parties where, by and large, the central bodies were

---

[57] Johnson, Charles, The Missoulian, May 30, 2012

[58] Ibid.

now working to their own regional organizations of party members. As these parties grew very large, so they fell into the hands of professional party officials. This, said Roberto Michaels, was the inevitable consequence of all large-scale organizations. The party might well claim and indeed think itself to be democratic, its members might well think that it was they who made policy. In fact, it was nothing of the sort. The party had fallen prey, as all large-scale organizations must, to oligarchy. 'Who says organization, says oligarchy.' And the party was, in reality, a 'following' behind a small group of party professionals who evolved the party's policy and then set out to get the mass membership to endorse it."[59]

Was it the entire Republican Party that decided gay marriage was an election-year issue in the fall of 2004 to distract voters from thinking too much about the failings in Iraq? Until that time it was a non-issue. A handful of party operatives, including Karl Rove made it an issue, and then set it upon the party faithful who drowned out any shortcomings of the incumbent President with this well-timed distraction.

Was it every member of Democratic Party that decided Sen. Barack Obama should run against Sen. Hillary Clinton for the Democratic presidential nomination? Sorry, it was a handful of Democratic Party operatives who made that call. Why? They didn't want Hillary to get the nomination. In the eyes of that chosen few, she was an upstart, a carpetbagger, and what is more important, she hadn't paid her political dues in the trenches of party politics long enough to satisfy their agenda. That and the fact that she had polarizing baggage *before* she was elected.

The kind the Great Decider developed *after* he was elected told them she could lose the Independent vote, and cost the party the

[59] Finer, S.E., The History of Government, Vol. 3, Book V, Pathways to the Modern State, No. 5 Industrialization 6.6, Oxford University Press, 1997, p.1650-1651.

White House. They weren't going to take that chance, so they brought in the tele-genetic biracial candidate with the lovely spouse, and the rest, as they say, is history.

What did Hillary, the physical representation of the female majority of our population in America get out of this? Be a good girl Hill, take the secretary job, keep your nose clean, stay on message, and then we'll give you the nod for the presidency in 2016. Yes, America, that is how party politics works at that level.

To further emphasize the point, the year Hillary didn't get the party's nod Nancy Pelosi did as the top legislative position in the House of Representatives. Why? She worked the party trenches as a good foot soldier for decades. That was her hard-earned reward.

Several decades after women fought to win the right to vote and a few decades after they became the de facto majority of the American population, the Democratic Party finally got around to elevating and elect a woman to a position of real political power. Oh boy, break out the champagne! Making women wait that long is hardly what one would call a progressive and liberal agenda. A progressive and liberal agenda would have been to work steadily, year after year, purposefully encouraging and educating women to run for legislative and judicial positions throughout the country so that their percentages in both would be closer to reflecting their percentages of the actual population and workforce. Nothing close to that happened. Yes, there was some encouragement and training, but it fell far short of what was necessary for women to feel comfortable in being involved in what has increasingly become a contact sport. The king of the mountain, winning is everything mentality turn many women off and away from political participation.

With Democrats being the majority for so long—40 years in the house—there was no real motivation to bring women in the political ranks. Now that there are over eight million more registered women to vote in America than men, using the female vote to maintain and increase their political power has become tantamount to the Democrats pursuit of the majority. The Democrats primary motivation for this is not to see more women elected to office, but solely to regain the majority and stay in power. This from a party that got lazy, then became complacent. Complacent in their attitude, "We're the majority so take our superior ideas or leave it." Attitude brimming with political smugness of how right they were, how right they are, so there was no incentive to bring in new blood, new ideas, or women into the fold.

It was after all, the Democrats who pushed a president from the White House and saved the nation, or so they would have us believe. So what if we lost the White House of the Great Communicator, we are right and we know it, and we still control Congress. Only after Republicans retook the majority in the House and Senate, and Democrats own self-righteous smugness was met by the Republicans and Rush Limbaugh's, I'm right about everything and you're an idiot Amer-o-gant attitude, did the Democrats start getting serious about courting women for their political ranks. The same way the Republicans coerced and used the religious right to rebuild their base after being humiliated in the aftermath of the Democrats driving Nixon from the White House.

National politics being what it is, Republicans waited 25 years for the political payback by impeaching the Great Philanderer in the House. In 2005, Andy Shaw of ABC Channel 7 news Chicago interviewed then retiring Congressman Henry Hyde from DuPage County, Illinois and asked him if impeaching Clinton was, in part, political revenge against the Democrats for forcing Nixon out.

"Was this a payback?" asked Shaw.

"I can't say that it wasn't," responded Congressman Hyde.[60]

Both parties are a joke, with the Republican Party being far worse, when it comes to promoting the political prominence of women, minority parties, minorities, and Independents. Oligarchies don't do competition. Political monopolies don't do competition, and they openly say so. The quotes in Chapter one from the heads of the DNC and RNC are only two examples of what goes on within the parties about not wanting or having competition. When Rep. Jefferson-D-MS, was found with $98,000 in his freezer, the Democrats did nothing to support a challenge to his re-election from an African American female state legislator within the party. The parties are always there to support their members and make sure we never forget why con is in the word Congress.

In holding back women, the parties continue to alienate them and drive them away. The same can be said of minority party members and minorities. Steadily over time, voters trickle away from Democrats and Republicans. Like the dripping of the proverbial Chinese water torture it drives the major parties nuts, and they try even harder to exercise their control over the voters and elections. It isn't working.

Even the current President recognizes this. In January 2010, the Great Yes We Can, in addressing Republicans at a retreat during talks on health care reform, had this to say, "Let me close by saying this. I was not elected by Democrats or Republicans, but by the American people. That is especially true because the fastest-growing group of Americans are independents. That should tell us both something."[61]

[60] Shaw, Andy, ABC Channel 7 News Chicago, Interviewing Rep. Henry Hyde April 22, 2005.

[61] President Barrack Obama, C-Span, Speech to Republicans, January 29, 2010, m.18:37.

That should tell Democrats and Republicans everything they need to know, but they are not listening. Americans, the majority being women, continue to move forward politically without them. Why aren't the parties listening? Because of the ongoing backdoor corporate intervention in the politics of democracy that continues to steamroll through Washington D.C. on a daily basis.

Corporate America is the boys club, where women aren't allowed. At least that's what they hope for. Grudgingly, they let the gals in, but at a pace that makes an ESPN slow-motion highlight look like it's moving at the speed of light. The corporate intervention in politics is, in style and substance, a latter-day version of the military intervention in politics during the French Revolution by the military.

Again from Samuel Finer's History of Government, "However, 'military intervention' admits of several degrees. One might range these in a spectrum. At one pole the army is acting constitutionally 'in aid of the civil power.' However, as government comes to depend on its support, *the army* may use the government dependency to blackmail it. This can develop into, effectively, military *indirect* rule, that is to say directing the politics of the government from behind-the-scenes, including evicting the government for a more compliant one."[62] Change the words military and army into Wall Street bankers, energy companies, or defense contractors and the connection is clear.

My phrasing, However, as government comes depend on its support, the [*Wall Street bankers*] may use the government dependency to blackmail it. This can develop into, effectively [*Wall Street bankers*] *indirect* rule, that is to say directing the politics of the government from behind the scenes, including evicting government for a more compliant one.

---

[62] Finer, S.E., The History of Government, Vol. 3, Book V, Pathways to the Modern State, No. 3 Legacy of the French Revolution, 8.1.3, Oxford University Press, 1997, p. 1560.

Is this what Sen. Dick Durbin meant when he said, "And they frankly own the place,"[63] in response to reporters questions about the lobbying strength of Wall Street financial institutions in the U.S. Senate that helped defeat a bill Sen. Durbin sponsored to help stem foreclosures in early 2009?

 The constant need to sell treasury bonds on a massive scale for decades is how Wall Street supported the government, and how the government came to depend on them to do so, allowing Wall Street to blackmail the government when the time was ripe. When the U.S. House of Representatives initially voted not to pass the TARP bailout in October 2008, Wall Street's response was a one day 787 point drop in the Dow. Effectively putting Washington D.C. on notice—give us the cash or we'll sink this ship and you'll take the blame.

 When former Federal Reserve chief Paul Volker quit in disgust as head of the Great Yes We Can's Council on Jobs and Competitiveness and was replaced by GE's Jeffrey Immelt, this was evicting the government for a more compliant one. Saying or alluding to the fact that Immelt is on the same level as Volker in understanding the complexities of the economy, regulation, and how they work individually and together, is to say or allude to the idea that heavenly Senator Ted Cruz-sader, R-Hallelujah, and Einstein are equals in understanding relativity theory. It was Volker after all who made it clear that the greatest feat of financial engineering over the last 30 years was the ATM machine. Everything else, according to the former Federal Reserve chief, was smoke and mirrors and did nothing to improve the national economy. The same smoke and mirrors Immelt indulged in while running GE off a financial cliff and into the government's pocket for cool $75 billion within several

---

[63] Senator Durbin, Richard, http://progressillinois.com/2009/4/29/durbin-banks-own-the-place, April 29, 2009.

months of the start of the financial crisis. As the Wall Street Journal reported, "GE is lucky it was too big to fail, or it might have failed as smaller business lender CIT did."[64]

Mr. Immelt is the fine fellow who was interviewed by Charlie Rose in 2012, and when speaking about our government v. the Chinese government, he quipped, "State run communism may not be your cup of tea, but their government works."[65] Perhaps he forgot that when business leaders like himself, who nearly run a company into the ground, and in doing so nearly wreck the country's economy, do so in China, they are either jailed for life or executed in front of a firing squad. Be careful what you wish for Mr. Immelt.

The corporate political creed is my way or the highway. Publicly, few on Wall St. are better at conveying this mentality than Jamie Dimon, head of JP Morgan Chase. Commenting on former Fed. Chair Paul Volker's comments about large banks "Mr Dimon responded that he had just two words to describe them: "infantile" and "nonfactual."[66] "But it appears to have been a classic performance from Mr. Dimon. In your face. Pugnacious. My way or the highway."[67] It reflects the Darwinist barbarianism of, to the victor goes the spoils, mentality of corporate structure and hierarchy.

Interviewed in *Barron's* in June 2012, Simon Mikhailovich stated the obvious about the dealings of banks like JP Morgan Chase, "If you were offered a game of chance where when you win, you win, and when you lose, you are given another chance to throw the dice, then, of course, everybody would play that game and

[64] Review and Outlook, Wall Street Journal, The Fed's Bailout Files, December 2, 2010.

[65] Immelt, Jeffery, CBS News, The Immelt Interview, December 10, 2012, http://www.realclearpolitics.com/video/2012/12/11/jeff_immelt_chinas_ communist_ government _works.html, 00:44 sec.

[66] Morgenson, Gretchen, The New York Times, Sunday Business, May 13, 2012, p.1.

67 Ibid, p.1 and 6.

essentially that is where the financial system is. That isn't capitalism."[68]

Of course it's not capitalism, it's circle jerk cronyism, with the participants performing financial felatio on one another to keep the party going. Something the leaders of big banks and many members of Congress are very skilled at. Oligarchy is written all over this way of thinking. As mentioned earlier, it is the very few setting policy for the many to follow. The same philosophy promoted and used by Republicans since the inception of the previously mentioned Republican Con Act with America.

Electing the first MBA president, the Great Decider, shows how high up the political landscape this corporate intervention is moving along. The fact that big corporate money was behind the Great Flipper, Mitt Romney, the former private equity CEO, to be the Republican nominee, shows the promoters of the corporate intervention want nothing less than one of their own in the White House. For who better to promote the corporate and Republican dogma of lower taxes, less government, and less regulation, than those who stand to gain the most from fleecing the U.S. Treasury? We all understand it is their campaign contributions (read: legalized bribery) to members of both parties that keeps the parties under their control, in power, and political competition nonexistent.

We all understand that in betting on a horse race, the fewer the horses, the easier it is to bet on all the horses because, naturally, it requires less money to cover a two horse race than a 15 horse race. Political horse races are no different. A 15 candidate presidential horse race, like the Swiss have, as mentioned in Chapter 1, might cause Super Pacs to blow a fuse in the general election because they would need 15 times the cash to cover all

---

68 Blumenthal, Robyn, Barron's, Interview with Simon Mikhailovich, June 4, 2012, p.42.

the bets to ensure they put money on the winner. This competition may well price the richest donors out of the market.

Imagine the Koch brothers, their followers (Kochheads), and the politicians that suck up to them for their money (Kochsuckers), being neutralized by political competition. That is what multiple party and Independent candidates would do the political marketplace. Republicans talk endlessly of the need to roll back or eliminate government restrictions in the marketplace. How about rolling back or eliminating government restrictions to ballot access put upon the populace by the Democrats and Republicans on the state and federal level to increase those political horses in the race?

As the race grows, so grows democracy. The more people participate as candidates, the more people participate in democracy. Look what happened in the aftermath of the California Gubernatorial recall in 2003. A wide open Republican primary, one the party had no control over, garnered 130 entrants into the primary horse race. Competition means everyone has to work harder. Competition enhances creativity. Competition brings out the best and worst in human beings.

What could be worse than that? No competition at all. No competition enforces and promotes the *Myway-highway* philosophy. That philosophy is the antithesis of democracy. A democracy, which in its essence, is like Einstein's relativity. No matter what your point of view or point of observation, all views are valid, and equally so. Einstein's relativity theory was, and is, the scientific validation of a core element of democracy; no one vote being greater than, or more important than another, all votes relative to one another. Most people think Einstein's greatest contribution to humanity was in the field of physics. Intended or not, his scientific theories confirm what humanity had fought, died, and dreamed of for centuries: the individual as valid and equal participant in the governing over their affairs, equal to those of their fellow citizens to do the same.

"And the sound spirit of legislation, which, banning all arbitrary and unnecessary restraint on individual action, shall leave us free to do whatever does not violate the equal rights of another." Thomas Jefferson–1818 [69]

Einsteinian Democracy or Darwinist Corporatocracy, which would you have your children and grandchildren learn and live by? Good old boy corporate America doesn't do everybody's equal philosophy. They practice another kind of philosophy. The invasion of this philosophy, like a cancer invading a body, in this case the body politic, is displayed in one of its clearest examples with the political, then corporate, and then further political rise of Deficits Don't Matter Dick Cheney. Deferment Dick was too busy doing other things, like rising to become presidential Chief of Staff, to do anything else back in the 1960s and 1970s. Then corporate America got a hold of him in Halliburton, where he learned the *Myway-highway* mindset of some, but not all CEOs of large corporations. Then Deferment Dick went back to government as Vice President where his newfound philosophy could be practiced and inflicted upon the democratic system of compromising to achieve consensus. The former VP's Dick-tater style was stamped on everything he did and everything he said. The most obvious and visible statement of his style was on the floor of the U.S. Senate in the words, "Fuck yourself,"[70] declaration to Sen. Patrick Leahy.

What followed was more of the same. Don't like our Middle-East policy? Don't like us doing things The U.S. Supreme Court

---

[69] Jefferson, Thomas, Report of the Commissioners for the University of Virginia, 1818 Lapham's Quarterly, Vol. 1 No. 4, Fall, 2008 p.28.

[70] Dewer, Helen; Milbank, Dana, The Washington Post, Cheney Dismisses Critic With Obscenity, June, 25, 2004, p.A 4.

has ruled unconstitutional? Don't like the fact that we are funding day-to-day life on borrowed money? Hey, FY! Is it any wonder why the average American is developing the same attitude towards elected officials and their own government? It is the economic trickle-down theory morphing into the *Myway-highway* philosophy. Yes, monkey see, monkey do.

The invasion of Iraq by the U.S. is a further example of the ever-expanding behind-the-scenes influence of the corporate doctrine. Many called it the Bush doctrine, when it was and is the corporate doctrine. Right out of the corporate textbooks on how to implement a successful hostile corporate takeover.

1. Make your offer to the outfit you wish to fleece; in this case the country of Iraq.

2. After negotiations break down you make your move; sending in the M&A boys, originally Mergers and Acquisitions, now the Marines and Army.

3. You remove the current CEO and board; Saddam Hussein and the Baath party

5. You install your own CEO; Paul Brenner, and a new board; Chalabi and his counterfeiting cronies, later replaced by Malaki and his.

5. Create massive layoffs; civil servants and army

6. Peel away many existing assets; priceless antiquities.

7. Eliminate as many non-performing assets as you can; the citizens.

8. Spruce up the performing assets; oil.

9. Handicap the country with horrendous debt; destroyed infrastructure.

10. Skim 10 percent of the total buyout cash into your friends pockets.

Congratulations you've just graduated from the school of hostile corporate takeovers. Time to send the M&A boys home. As with all hostile corporate takeovers this one was done with borrowed money. Money borrowed from a bank. A bank commonly known as the U.S. taxpayer.

This is what we did to Iraq. Still want to call it a war?

If that isn't enough, how about the fact that over a decade later the Chinese now import half of Iraq's oil, and they never fired a shot. "We lost out,"said Michael Makovsky, a former Defense Department official in the Bush Administration who worked on Iraq oil policy. "The Chinese had nothing to do with the war, but from an economic standpoint they are benefiting from it, and our Fifth Fleet and air forces are helping to assure their supply."[71]

The continued influence of the *Myway-highway* being built by corporate America has paved its way to the Republican Party. It is now the mantra of the party on the state and federal level. It is causing moderates in the party to become nonexistent as they get steamrolled and run over by the proponents of this attitude in the party. The unease in this *Myway-highway* getting bigger and paving over even more of the political landscape is its close relationship to absolutism. What is absolutism? The embryonic stages of fascism.

Yes, it's a long haul between the two, but the continued travel down this road continues to bring them closer together with every passing decade. Unlike the majority of the rest of the world where some form of absolutism or fascism has existed in their respective political histories, we in America are too young a nation to have experienced a totalitarian government. So in our

---

[71] Arango, Tim and Krauss, Clifford, The New York Times, China is Reaping Biggest Benefits of Iraq Oil Boom, June 2, 2013

youthful naiveté we don't, and perhaps won't, recognize fascism in America when we first see it. For what nation's inhabitants ever recognize fascists at first sight? Rarely, long after it has grown and established itself, do people wake up to the horrors of it. Just ask the Germans. Did they see the Nazis for what they were at their inception?

Similarly in America, will we recognize our own fascists? Will we recognize our own Nazis, the Not-Sees? With all the Not-Sees in America today, do we understand that it is the Not-Sees that are the foot soldiers of America's homegrown version of fascism and American Not-Seeism. Yes, those that will Not-See that the two-party system is crushing American democracy, Not-See Americans yearning for a freer and more open political marketplace, Not-See the great lower taxes, less government, bigger military lie for what it is, Not-See that holding women back, politically, is causing undue harm to our form of government, and lastly Not-See that any nation that has seen civil war in its history will see civil war again if it fails to recognize the cause of the previous Civil War.

The cause of the previous Civil War? According to Civil War expert and filmmaker Ken Burns it was slavery and anyone that doesn't agree with his opinion doesn't know what they're talking about. The impression one gets from reading history is that the *issue* was slavery, but the *cause* was when people became so polarized, so partisan in their points of view, they were unable or unwilling to see another's point of view, and the nation went to war with itself. Yes, it took decades to come to a head, but it was the partisanship and the polarization of the issue of slavery that caused the Civil War. In reality the reason we don't recognize Not-Seeism isn't that we have not experienced an element of it in the past, it is that no one is alive to remember its horrors and how it devastated the nation.

Fortunately it did not result in anything worse than a pause in our walking towards the horizon of democracy.

Think about the polarization that it took the nation to fight itself, then look at the polarization growing annually in American politics today. A polarization brought on, in a major way, by the two-party system. This is not my own point of view but those of many elected officials and lobbyists I have spoken to over the last two decades.

The majority will tell you that civility is evaporating at a rapid rate everywhere. Today they will tell you that twenty years ago, legislative committee members, regardless of party affiliation, conferred, dined, and compromised together all the time to make and pass legislation. Today? Members on the same committee don't even speak to one another based on party.

Look at that growth in partisanship over the last two decades practiced by the Democrats and Republicans. Now project that out another 20 years, and another 20 years after that. Where is this taking us? Look at all the Not-Sees around you solidly on the right, and gaining speed on the left, unwilling to change or compromise their points of view. Where is this leading us? Where is this growing Not-Seeism going to take us? A prime example of this was two bumper stickers I saw on two different cars within 15 minutes of one another belonging to modern day American Not-Sees. On the first car; Profit is Theft, and on the second car; Evolution is Science Fiction. How are you going to get compromise out of people like that?

There is an ancient Chinese tale in which there are two scorpions in a box. Knowing the nature of the scorpion is to attack and destroy, the question is asked, how do you keep the two scorpions from stinging each other to death? The answer; you add a third scorpion. That way none will attack the other, always wary of the other two. The destructive nature of the scorpion now becomes one of compromise to survive. The same compromise that moved the U.S. Capital from Philadelphia to present Washington D.C. The same compromise that caused Washington D.C. to be shaped like a diamond.

It was compromising that had the founders of the United States add a third, equally powerful branch to the new government being formed, so that two alone would not annihilate one another. This was the concern that formed the basis for three equally powerful branches to the new government in Revolutionary America. Compromise is the lifeblood of American democracy helping it survive as long as it has in the walk toward that horizon. The compromise women do so much better than men when it comes to everyday life, culturally and politically. Realistically speaking, we men compromise, but women *accommodate*. Do you know the difference?

Politically today we have red states and blue states. Hey America, how many colors to our flag? What ever happened to red, white, and blue states? Three branches of government, three colors to the flag, each separate but equal. How about adding a third color, separate but equal, to our political spectrum to make it even stronger? In adding another color, let that color be the color of women. Women of all colors expanding the vision and strength of our democratic political spectrum.

Chapter 3

I'd rather regret the things I have done, than the things that I haven't-
Lucille Ball

In America today there is only one analogy that I can think of that can be properly used to describe the modern women's political movement: a bowel movement. That's right it stinks. It stinks to high heaven, stinks out loud. Bad enough that women get caught up in the Democrat-Republican, conservative-liberal shell game while being the slight majority in populace and workplace, but then you go out and follow the man trap of trying to play the King of the Mountain game where winning is everything. Ladies how did you allow yourself to be duped into thinking this was and is your way to political power? Sure it works for us guys, we're wired for that kind of thinking and acting out that type of thought process, but you, you're wired for something different. That something different is sharing and accommodating along with your desire to get ahead.

Women see differently than men, too. They see colors better and with better visual acuity. Men see the peripheral better, better too in low light. This was all laid out quite effortlessly one day in the early 1990s on a boat ride from the United States to Canada. The ferry ride from Port Angeles, Washington to Victoria, British

Columbia on a beautiful spring day is a great place to brush up on your human physiology if you happen to be lucky enough to run into a chemist named Judy Donegan. We met about the time the ferry had churned out of Port Angeles Harbor past the tip of Ediz Hook into the open waters of the Strait of Juan de Fuca streaming in from the Pacific Ocean. The Strait that separates the furthest northwest portion of the mainland United States from the largest island in the eastern Pacific. Vancouver Island buffering the incoming Pacific swells from the mainland of British Columbia, with its provincial capital of Victoria, lay dead ahead off our bow.

Behind us, the glacial covered peaks and conifer rain forests of Olympic National Park slipped away at our stern when our introduction began. Judy was on her way home.

"And where's home?"

"Joyzee", she replied in that dialectic style only a native could live and breathe.

"You're taking a circuitous route to put it mildly."

"Yes," she said, "I wanted to see more of the country so I drove from California and after I see Victoria and Vancouver, I'll head east."

Judy had been living in Lo Cal, Los Angeles, for a couple of years. She'd been sent there by her employer, the Kodak company, to set up the company's sole West Coast developing lab. A chemist by training, Judy had run the company's New Jersey lab for years, and Kodak wanted one in Lo Cal, so Judy from Joyzee went west. Now she was going home.

"So how'd you like living in California?"

"I loved the place. The climate was so nice but the people, they drove me nuts!", she exclaimed eyes rolling skyward with a look of disbelief.

"They did?"

"Oh my God, those people," said she now getting quite animated with her hands, "they are so laid back, so mellow. I can't do mellow. I can do a lot of things, but I can't do mellow. Oh my God please, not mellow, anything but mellow!", she continued, throwing her arms up in the air with a look of exasperation that could only come from a Joyzee native trying to figure out if she was still in the United States or had moved to an alien culture dealing with Lo Cal's finest.

"Somebody had to go and I was the only one who could mix the chemicals for the lab."

"Why?" I asked.

"Because women have more cones than men in the structure of their eyes, so we see color more acutely. To have the proper colors, real-life colors when developing Kodachrome you need a woman to do the mixing of the various developing chemicals to ensure the outcome is right. Men don't see colors the way we do. Men have more rods than cones in their eyes structure so you have better peripheral and low light vision."

"Is this why we're better at driving at night?" I inquired.

"Exactly," she said continuing, "the irony being only men can be colorblind to varying degrees, and it can only be passed on to them from the mother. I work for Kodak mixing the chemicals for the Kodachrome because it is the film that shows human skin tone better than anything."

"Still?" I asked.

"Yes, it's why the fashion industry still uses it and it alone. They shoot tens of thousands of roles annually and it all ends up in our lab in New Jersey. That's why Kodak sent me to LA to set up a lab for the growing fashion and celebrity industry out there."

"Wow, so you're the go-to-gal for the fashion industry when it comes to film development."

"That's right," she said, "like I said before, women can see colors in ways you can't. It's the way we evolved together. Women were the gatherers in the daytime, and men were the hunters at dusk and dawn. It's one of the ways men and women came to depend on one another to survive."

Evolving together, becoming dependent on one another out of necessity to survive. This exposes one of the most odorous and putrid saying to come out of the politics-bowel movement mentioned at the start of this chapter, a woman needs a man like a fish needs a bicycle.

When Geneva Overholser wrote her column, *French strike a Blow for Feminism*, in April 2001 she interviewed Edith Crisson, the first woman prime minister of France. Edith Crisson had this to say about feminism, "The difference between French and American feminism is that French men and women like and need each other."[72]

This could be because, as cultures go, France passed the prepubescent stage long ago. You know, the girls are yucky, eewww the boys are yucky stage we all went to in our younger years. Nations go through it too.

"One nation is to another what one individual is to another,"[73] When James Madison wrote those words in Federalist 62, he was onto something. Something in our modern instant gratification world we rarely remember, that nations like people, grow and mature over time. Part of that growing up is being more accepting of the world around us.

Accepting that while the attitude of the battle of the sexes may have been childish fun in the rebellious 1960s, now that many baby boomers are in their 60s, isn't it about time we grew up

[72] Overholser, Geneva, Seattle Post-Intelligencer, Washington Post Writers Group, French Strike a Blow for Feminism, April 25, 2001.

[73] Madison, James as Publius, The Federalist Papers, Number 62, February 27, 1788.

from that infantile mindset? Isn't it about time men and women accept the fact that we need each other, not just socially, but politically too? Oh I see, too French for you? You wouldn't be caught dead emulating those pompous socialists right?

Of course you wouldn't. Who in their right mind would want to imitate the folks who imitated our lead in revolution over 200 years ago? Imitate a group of lazy cheese eating surrender monkeys who would give the gift of a Roman Goddess? Are you nuts? So what if the Roman Goddess was Libertas, embodied as a statue, Liberty Enlightening the World. Yes, those galling DeGaullists had the nerve to plunk her down right smack dab in the middle of New York Harbor, where everyone entering by boat or plane would have to see that woman.

Let's face it, it is sooo French. A real red-blooded American statue would have been nothing of the kind. No way. A real American statue, one that reflected real American manliness the kind Duke Wayne and Dutch Reagan lived by, would have been a guy with a backward baseball cap on his head, pants hanging halfway down the crack of his ass, can of beer cradled in his left hand, right arm reaching skyward, with his index finger and pinky extended, and exclaiming, "Duuuuuuude let's Paaaarty!"

Thank goodness the French didn't go that route. Thank goodness it was the gift of Lady Liberty the French bestowed upon us to celebrate our Centennial. A woman lighting the way to a better world for which everyone was hoping, dreaming would be their own under her watchful eyes. Which brings us back to that vision thing. With women being able see colors better, clearer than men, it means women can see the entire spectrum of color in ways we men cannot. Which leads, naturally, to women seeing the entire spectrum of life in ways we men cannot. With the ability to see the colors of life differently, clearer if you will, what type of clarity of vision can women bring our nation when they become equal partners not just in population and workplace but all things legislative and judicial within the governing of this nation? A nation that uses a Roman Goddess to define a cornerstone of her beliefs. No, it was never Mister, Herr, Señor, or Monsieur Liberty, it is Lady, thank you, and she is not alone. Her dear friend and sister Roman Goddess Justitia, Lady Justice, is right there next to her, up front and center in the American psyche.

With Liberty and Justice for All.[74]

 Two women who symbolize the foundation of what our country is built on, what we all live for, and our combat veterans have laid down their lives for. Their names are etched in our individual and collective subconscious. We, with hand over heart, have been praising them, reciting them, before we ever understood the meaning of praising or reciting. Two women, one with torch and tablet, the other with scales and sword, defining a people, defining a nation.

 Unfortunately the two Grande Dames of American democracy have had a rough go of it lately. We used the excuse of September 11, 2001 to gang rape both of them mercilessly. Giving it to them from all sides. Yes, it was their fault for being so open, so liberal, so fair, and so alluring. They deserved it. They asked for it. We used words like extraordinary rendition, enemy combatant, insurgent, and of course, insertion to justify our actions in making these harlots submit to correcting their coercive powers.

 Our collective condemnation of their graceful beauty and wisdom to be out of fashion for the times became the norm. Our

---

[74] Last line of the Pledge of Allegiance to the Flag of The United States of America.

collective condom-nation, sheathing ourselves from their wanton ways was displayed nowhere better than former U.S. Attorney General John Ashcroft. The right-hand, or was it right wing man of the Great Decider during his first administration.

Mr. Ashcroft was the result of the Midwest upbringing. Ah the Midwest, legendary for its sensibilities. Where else but America's heartland do they sensibly allowed dead people to vote (Chicago) and vote dead people into office (Missouri)?

On the latter remember, in the 2000 election, the guy without the pulse, Mel Carnahan, beat the incumbent U.S. Senator with the pulse, John Ashcroft, to become the new-deceased U.S. Senator from the state whose motto is "Salus Populi Suprema Lex Esto," or "Let the Welfare of the People be Supreme Law." Missourians sensibly thought the guy without a pulse would be better, "Welfare of the People," than John 'Burqa' Ashcroft. Ashcroft became the only incumbent elected official in U.S. history to lose to a dead guy. And people think the Chicago Cubs are the biggest losers in the Midwest?

The Great Decider then decided to make him the country's Attorney General. When Burqa Ashcroft entered the Department of Justice he became so tit-elated at the sight of Lady Justice's naked breast, he had her robed, or was it robbed, of her Justitian beauty. While many, including the man himself, stated that the reason she was covered was the indecency of her bare breast, in reality it was the sight of her equally balance scales of justice that unhinged the man. Scales that would not allow his own self-righteous religious dogma to tip the scales in favor of his favored few. So what could he do? Cover them! Out of his sight, out of his mind. The latter being an accurate assessment of his legal proxies during the nearly eight years of Justitia's burqa detention.

Have Libertas's and Justitia's ageless beauty and indispensable wisdom really gone out of fashion? Just listen to a woman of the Arab spring, Mehrezia Labidi of Tunisia, and the highest ranking elected female in the Arab world, writing in the Guardian: "Far from being neutral passive spectators, Arab women, from Tunisia to Syria, and in all Arab cities where people have gone out–and are still going out–to demand their rights to freedom and dignity have been actively participating in all stages, levels, and fields of the revolution. They have planned, demonstrated, reached to the outside world; they have been injured and killed."[75] Injured and killed chasing after, and reaching for, something we in America, women included, regularly take for granted, our freedoms and our rights.

Ms. Labidi continued, " Women constitute almost 28 percent of our assembly. Whether in the opposition or in the three parties represented in the coalition government, women in the assembly are real actors. They are represented in each of the six constituent commissions. One of the most important of these, the rights and liberties commission, is headed by a woman: the lawyer, human rights activists, and former victim of torture, Farida Labidi."[76]

American women make up under twenty percent of the federal legislature, but in newly democratic Tunisia they are 28 percent. For America, for American women, this is a national embarrassment. A country whose informational, monetary, and political resources of their newly formed democracy pale in comparison to our own, yet they can accomplish in a couple of years what we have been unable to achieve in over 200 years, getting 28 percent of our federal legislative positions to be held by women.

---

[75] Labidi, Mehrezia, The Guardian, http://www.guardian.co.uk/commentisfree/2012/mar/23/tunisia-women-revolution?INTCMP=SRCH, March 23, 2012.

[76] Ibid.

Notice that Ms. Labidi mentions a three party coalition to achieve a majority to an opposition. Newly created Tunisian democracy is diverse enough for four major parties, but America is only diverse enough for two major parties? Who are they kidding?

Mrs. Labidi continues, nailing down what helped women achieve such democratic advances. "The Arab revolutions have created a space for women to participate as never before, but achieving real change in our reality demands unity and vision. The great expectations of our people and the immense sacrifices they have made compel us to cooperate. This is not a matter for parties or ideologies."[77]

Hear that women of America? Time to jettison the party line, the ideology, if you wish to find unity among yourselves to achieve your rightful place in American government, the majority. Yes, women of America look at what you have collectively in resources to achieve this. What's stopping you? Men? Grow up, that is so 1960s. Is it the fear of failure, or is it the fear of success? A success that would carry the weight, the burden of responsibility of being equal partners and perhaps the majority. Be it your fate, be it your destiny, call it what you will, majority rule is the law of the land, and you are the majority. When are you going to take hold of the reins of political power and help guide this continuous ride towards that horizon of democracy?

Have I missed something here? Being a guy, is my vision not so clear after all? Is it not your fear of failure or fear of success that hold women back? Something else? Might it be the self-imposed chains of complacency? Those chains of complacency many of us, myself included, have fastened upon ourselves in our ever so comfortable lives in America. Ours is quite comfortable compared to those who have participated in and died during

---

[77] Ibid.

extended Arab Spring to get a taste of what we, men and women in America, get to overindulge in daily. Yes, there are plenty of women out there, all around us, who are up for the task of looking and acting beyond the partisan puff. We've had them right in front of us, in high government positions nonetheless, yet they never garner much of our attention personally or collectively, because they were not front and center spinning the conservative-liberal shell game.

 Do you remember Brooksley Born? Ever even heard of her? There she was, in the late 1990s, running the Commodities Futures Trading Commission. In 1998 she wrote a paper expressing the idea of looking into the possibility, repeat only looking into the possibility, of regulating financial derivatives. She became concerned because of the folding of Long Term Capital Management (LTCM) in that year. Their trillions of dollars in derivatives contracts were backed by mere billions in real assets. She was worried that this fairly new and unregulated market would cause much bigger problems to the financial system in the future. She was in charge of futures, so her concerns seem reasonable.

 Enter the Committee that Saved the World, or so Time magazine exclaimed in its title page in the aftermath of the LTCM debacle. There they were, the financial Three Stooges of our time, Moe, Larry, and Curly, a.k.a. Rubin, Summers, and Greenspan, gracing the cover. Oh yes we heard about how great they were, how they, "Saved" us from financial melt down. What we didn't read or learn is how the Three Stooges, with the help of Arthur Levitt, Security and Exchange Commission Chairman, literally ran Ms. Born out of D.C. for writing her paper on derivatives. They went before Congress to ensure laws would be enacted to prevent any regulation of derivatives. They collectively worked against Ms.

Born. Her reward? She was forced out and resigned, no longer having the support of her boss.

Within the year of her sacking, Democratic Sen. Byron Dorgan D–ND, would give a speech on the Senate floor that would prove prophetic when he denounced the repeal of the Glass–Steagall Act in November 1999. He said within 10 years America would regret the day. Did Moe, Larry, Curly, and Levitt gang up on him the way they did Ms. Borne, and try to drive him from office for speaking out in public against something they supported? Hardly. His reward? The former senator now lives the good life with his senatorial pension.

How did Levitt and the Three Stooges fair? Levitt went on to the Carlyle Group, and wrote a book titled, TAKE ON THE STREET: What Wall Street and Corporate America Don't Want You to Know/What You Can Do to Fight Back.

Why not, FLAKE ON THE BEAT: What Wall Street and Corporate America Don't Want You to Know. How I Kissed Special Interest Patootie longer than anyone at the SEC/Now you're stuck with the Tab.

Moe Rubin, former head of Golden Sacks, moved on to the board of Citibank which caved again, the second time in less than 20 years, from management idiocy. Larry Summers moved on to Harvard, only to be run out and into The Great Yes We Can's wild bunch. What of Curly?

Ah yes, Curly Greenspan, former head of the Federal Reserve, a job he attained after some typical Curly hi-jinks elevated his profile. That being the bagman and promoter to Mr. Charles Keating [78], rhymes with cheating, lead singer and founder of the legendary senatorial rock band, The Keating Five.[79] Greenspan

---

78 Convicted Savings & Loan operator who cost taxpayers $2.5 billion. Alan Greenspan's employer before Greenspan became head of the Federal Reserve.

79 Democratic Senators Cranston, DeConcini, Glen, Riegle, and Republican Senator McCain took money to promote Keating's scam.

did such a fine job of promotion that the group's first and only album, Savings and Loan, went to the top of the charts. It then continued to blow up the charts, costing taxpayers billions. His reward, as we mentioned before: Chair of the Federal Reserve. Nice work if you can get it.

Another woman who was front and center, but most of us never paid attention to, was Sheila Bair. She was too busy running the Federal Deposit Insurance Corporation, FDIC, to be playing the conservative-liberal shell game before the cameras. She was playing another game. That game was, Stop the Foreclosures. In the fall of 2008, while Sarah Palin was working with her staff fashioning a wardrobe to elevate her status in the eyes of the public, Sheila Bair was working with her staff fashioning a plan to elevate homeowners out of foreclosure.

The plan she and her staff devised was to bring lenders and borrowers together to stop foreclosures from escalating to crisis proportions. She went to the Great Decider and Treasury Secretary Paulson, and asked for $25 billion in TARP money to get the program going. They turned her down. They turned down a program that likely would have stopped foreclosures nationwide. No longer able to help homeowners the way she wanted the FDIC to be able to, she kept working and did something unprecedented for a government employee. She had the staff of the FDIC post the entire program on the FDIC's website for everyone to see.

We the people, in the fall of 2008, had the template for successfully stopping home foreclosures on a state-by-state basis right in front of our eyes and we never saw it. We were too busy watching Sarah here, Sarah there, and Sarah everywhere, playing hockey mom, mama grizzly, and Republican Vice Presidential candidate, all the while parroting the partisan party line.

Sheila wasn't even a footnote in the back of our minds. Nor was she and what she was trying accomplish in the minds of many of those we sent to Washington D.C. to represent us. Sheila Bair, a woman with more financial savvy than the Great Decider, Deficits Don't Matter Dick Cheney, and Golden Sacks Paulson combined.

Then of course there is Elouise Cobell, Yellow Bird Woman, the Blackfeet warrior. A woman with more financial backbone than three Presidents, five U.S. Treasury Secretaries, and seven sessions of Congress combined. Raised in the shadows of Chief, Never Laughs, Almost a Dog, Sinopah, Medicine Grizzly, Rising Wolf, and Going to the Sun. In that part of the state of Montana, on that part of the Blackfeet Reservation, depending on which side of the ridge you're standing on, the water rushing down the rocks flows either south into the Atlantic Ocean by the Gulf of Mexico, or north to the Arctic Ocean by Hudson's Bay. She was part of the tribe that saw its first skirmishes with the white man in 1806 with Capt. Meriwether Lewis's murder of young Blackfeet. One hundred and ninety years later she would continue that fight by suing the U.S. Government. She alleged it had stolen $176 billion from all the tribes in the United States by not keeping track of the mineral and grazing royalties plus interest owed the tribes for which the U.S. government had drawn up the contracts and signed around 150 years earlier.

One hundred fifty years of royalties and compounded interest that had not been paid to its rightful recipients. She fought that battle for over 16 years, through three administrations, and having two Treasury Secretaries held in contempt of court. One of those, previously mentioned Moe Rubin, who, while trashing Brooksley Born, okayed his underlings at the U.S. Treasury in 1998 to shred Indian Trust Account documents by the thousands until a federal judge threatened him with an arrest warrant.

All this was possible because Rubin's boss, the Great Philanderer, was preoccupied dancing the self gratification shuffle while the band played the Cuban Cigar Swing. Having never inhaled, an alleged $176 billion swindle by the U.S. Government over Native Tribes would be easy to miss.

This was the state of things that didn't get past Norman Mailer's sharp eyed view of the Great Philanderer, "His shame, if he has any, is that he has never been able to stand up to the big money. He is powerless before men of huge financial size. Face to face with such buckos, the wind dies and the proud flag on the flagship commences to droop. As Monica Lewinsky is to Bill Clinton, so is Clinton to the big money - just a kid trying to earn his presidential knee-pads."[80]

Despite the president's poor dance move, and the sleazy moves by the U.S. Treasury, Yellow Bird Woman carried on. Carried on after the Great Decider sacked the sitting judge because, according to the former president, he was too biased.

When the Great Yes We Can came along, the amount had been whittled down to $27 billion, the figure was further reduced to $3.4 billion, and the government conceded defeat. The largest settlement against the U.S. Government in U.S. history, achieved by the sheer determination and stamina of one woman. Within a month of Congress finally approving the settlement, a settlement held up for almost a year because the Republicans were whining about paying such an amount, Elouise Cobell was diagnosed with cancer. Six months later she would be dead, the settlement still tied up in court by lawsuits from four of the recipients.

When I decided to head over the Continental Divide on a rainy Saturday morning in October 2011 to pay my respects to Elouise I had no idea what to expect. When I reached the divide at Marias Pass, the same pass Capt. Lewis searched in vain for

---

[80] Mailer, Norman, The Seattle Times, Los Angeles Times Syndicate, September ?,1998.

before his murderous entanglement with the Blackfeet, the sky was clearing and new snow dusted the faces of Rising Wolf and Sinopah. By the time I made to Browning, it was a bright sunny day with a stiff south wind and Elvis, the King, playing on the radio in honor of Elouise. There at the newly built Browning High School were pickups and cars by the hundreds. People from all over the state, and from other parts of the country were coming to pay their respects to Elouise. Blackfeet, Crow, Assiniboine, Piegan, Navaho, and Seminole came to sing and praise their friend, their flesh and blood.

Attending also was the state's senior U.S. Senator, Max Baucus. Elouise called on him regularly to help with the tribes struggle, but typical of Sen. Baucus, he put legislative weight behind it only when it became politically expedient for him to do so. So it came as no surprise with Elouise's memorial service still going, he and his minders would get up and walk out of the service before the end. Along the way his minders, guiding him along like a child, would have him stop and shake hands with whoever they thought was important for him to acknowledge, disrupting the attention from the deceased to himself, and walking out like it was no great shakes to disrupt the service. With behavior like that, like many in this state, I'm *Maxed out* on Baucus's senatorial shenanigans.

No matter, Elouise, along with Elvis in the house, present as a life-size cutout, ruled the day. Even in her passing, her legacy lives on. She helped set up and charter the Blackfeet National Bank, the first as such on a reservation, and the first national bank wholly owned by a Native American tribe. She established another bank, a 'mini bank' as she called it. Her concern was that Native American children were financially illiterate, so she started a bank within the bank for tribal high school students in order to help teach them about handling money. Today that mini bank has over 1200 tribal students on reservations all over the country. Their combined savings are now over $1 million and growing.

 These women, Brooksley Born, Sheila Bair, and Eloise Cobell share the same qualities that millions of women in this country have. Qualities that seem to have fallen out of favor in today's in-your-face contact sport style of accomplishing one's tasks or goals. Those qualities that are counterpoint of the upfront bravado, often times phony bravado, that plays out daily in our male-dominated political culture.

 Susan Cain, writing in her book *Quiet* gave a comparison of the styles with the example of Rosa Parks and Martin Luther King Junior. "A formidable orator refusing to give up his seat on a segregated bus wouldn't have had the same effect as a modest woman who'd clearly prefer to keep silent but for the exigencies of the situation. And Parks didn't have the stuff to thrill crowd if she had tried to stand up and announce she had a dream, but with King's help, she didn't have to."[81] Those qualities Parks displayed carry less and less gravity in today's political battleground, sadly to the detriment of American democracy. Those qualities are more often associated with women, although that is changing, than with men.

 Sharron Angle, Michele Bachman, and Sarah Palin, are prime examples of women aping the in-your-face bravado of men. Look at their accomplishments, overall, to the women mentioned previously. Hillary Clinton was a practitioner of said in-your-face style, but she too has found it to be more effective in getting her message across, moving closer to her goals, by abandoning her former style for one which has propelled her higher to greater levels of respect worldwide.

[81] Cain, Susan, Quiet: The Power of Introverts in a World That Can't Stop Talking, **Crown Publishing Group**, 2012, p.3.

Both styles are necessary, as Susan Cain shows, for societies and cultures to move forward economically and politically. The lack of real movement, real forward progress, in continuing to develop democracy in America has been stalled by the dominance of the male way of doing business, doing politics.

All of this is made more difficult still by the fact that women have started aping and mimicking the male way in politics. Chasing after the presidency, for women, is like chasing their tails. It might seem fun at the time but it's a zero-sum game. For all it's talked about, the real power in any state or federal government doesn't lie in the executive branch. It only executes the laws made by the legislative branches on the state and federal levels. This simple fact is lost on most Americans as we constantly look at our "leaders" to lead us.

Constitutionally, it is only Congress that can declare war. All attempts by the executive branch to take that power from Congress have happened only because Congress has been more than willing to fawn off the responsibility. To give away what the Constitution makes clear is their power and theirs alone to perform. The legislature sets the budget. It controls the funding for all government. The executive branch cannot impeach the legislative branch, the judicial branch cannot impeach the legislative branch, but the legislative branch can impeach both the executive and judicial branch members at will. Knowing these simple facts shows how foolish women's attempt to emulate men in going for the king of the mountain position in government, the executive branch, truly is.

It shows how, for generations, with the help of the American version of feminism, women have been led down the wrong path to real political power. An idea reinforced by those aching to see Hillary as president. The idea that somehow women will have achieved, "Real power," by controlling the White House is as foolish as it gets. So what if there is a woman in the White House when Congress and the Courts are dominated by aged white males? How women in this country can't see this or understand this is beyond me.

A perfect example of this mindless mindset was put forth during the recent National Journal 2020 Conference. A conference aimed at getting woman to the White House by 2020. Speaking at the conference in one panel group were Rep. Debbie Wasserman-Schultz head of the Democratic National Committee and Republican Rep. Kathy McMorris-Rogers the highest ranking Republican woman in the house of Representatives.

During the discussion Rep. Wasserman-Shultz commented that sometime in the next three presidential races a woman would come to the White House and she said, "We need more women in the pipeline," and we have to get more women, "in the supply chain."[82] After hearing these comments I thought to myself am I listening to a woman speaking about getting more women into politics or am I listening to the CEO or a board member of a major corporation talking about his latest product? The fact that we now have the head of the Democratic National Committee, and a woman, speaking like a corporate CEO about women's involvement in politics, tells us everything we need to know about how much current members of Congress in the Democratic and Republican parties are emulating men in not only how they speak, but how they act politically. This type of talk will help women to a point in gaining political power, the point of being more male.

My emphasis on women being a realistic solution to our current political troubles relies on a simple fact; women are already so well-connected in the basic levels of society. Be it their book

---

82 Congresswoman Wasserman-Schultz, Deborah, http://www.c-span.org/Events/ Conference-Addresses-Role-of-Women-in-Politics-and-Economy/10737432414/, July 18, 2012.

clubs, maternity clubs, social clubs, or social networking, the fundamentals for them to be an organized force are already there. Back in 2001, Michael Moore's oversized liberalism just about got his new book, Stupid White Men, spiked. According to Mr. Moore, his publisher was pulling his new book because it was too critical of the Bush administration. It was released right before September 11, 2001. They told him to completely rewrite it or it would be pulled and he'd have to reimburse the publisher. Who stopped all of this? A female librarian.

According to Mr. Moore he was giving a talk about his book being canceled to a group back east and a librarian in the crowd took note. It turns out she went home, got on her computer, and logged on to the national librarian network she was a part of. She let all the librarians in the country know what was about to happen to his book. He has stated that because of that e-mail many of those librarians across the country requested a copy of the book, to the tune of over 10,000 book orders from the publisher. The next thing he knew he had a national bestseller on his hands and the publisher backed down from canceling the book. All because a woman spoke up and spoke out on a network she was already a part of.

Speaking of networks, have you ever taken the time to notice when you go to vote that the majority, if not all, of those running the polling station are women? Think about that. Suppose those women decided to network and get connected to one another throughout every polling station in the nation. Now imagine they're all connected and they decide not to staff the polling stations a day or two before the national election in protest of the inequality in our political system relating to the lack of women in government. It's doubtful an election would happen. You just could not get that many men together in that short of period to staff all those polling places where people vote. Goodbye female polling station staff, goodbye election. All the preening, posturing, and strutting of the mostly male candidates would get flattened out like a pancake because woman would say enough to the foolishness of this phony baloney dog and pony show. Could it happen? If I can imagine it, along with anyone else in this country, then it is possible.

 The emulating of the male way of doing business in two party politics is stupefying women in their ability to *be women*, not men, in politics. It has stagnated the expression of the feminine in our political system. The one sided male expression is the cause for many of our current problems.

 Simply put, a stasis has set in the body politic and the two-party obstruction is stagnating the flow of political liberty and freedom in our political bloodstream. The way the Stasi's [83] mindset obstructed political liberty and freedom at every turn in the former East Germany. How do we break out of this stasis, the Stasi's mindset, politically?

 Well, we could try another Civil War, that went over big in the 1860s. Back then it was the blue states versus the gray states. Today it is the blue states versus the red states. Back then the blue states liked color and saw color as a good thing, so they had color, and the gray states didn't like color, unless it was slave labor, making human freedom a gray area, so they went gray. Today the blue states still like color so they have color, and the red states are the gray states colorized. Colorized because they see red every time they remember that there is a person in the White House whose skin isn't white. Even though his mother and grandparents that raised him are as lily white as Deficits Don't Matter Cheney and his mama.

 It really isn't a good idea because the odds say the blue states would win again. Okay, so the red states have more guns and

83 Former East German Secret Police.

ammo stockpiled up and ready to go. Yes, they'd win the first few battles, but as the war dragged on, and this one would, then all the extra money the blue states send to the red states to supplement the maintaining of federally subsidized hurricane insurance, crop insurance, crop rotation payments not to grow stuff, federal highway funds to maintain the roads, education grants, etc., would stop. The red states would have to spend so much money just to shore up what they once had, at the blue states subsidized expense, they wouldn't have any money left to buy bullets. Game over.

We could go even deeper into our history and go the revolutionary route. The trouble is, the new version would have more of a resemblance to the French Revolution that our own. That's because we'd now be doing what they did over 200 years ago, overthrowing virtually all existing institutions and regimes. Yes, it'd be fun for a while executing all those government types and the rich. Who knows, maybe we might bring back the guillotine just to see a few fat cat's heads role. In the end though we'd probably follow the French down the path of history, which any red blooded American would never be caught doing, and end up with a dictator, à la Napoleon.

Seeing how we've had Dick-tater style in Nixon and Cheney, we wouldn't be breaking any new ground there. Besides if you've got to have a tater lead, better to have the real deal, Mr. Potato Head. Doubtful he would do any worse in office than Deferment Dick or I'm not a Crook Dick.

Clearly civil war and revolution are not the paths we wish to follow to get women on equal footing with men politically. We could do the democratic thing and vote them into office, but because we Americans lazily reelect the incumbent, regardless of performance, over 80 percent of the time, this would take another century or longer to get the proper representation regarding population.

Term limits won't help either. Even though they are perceived to be a good way for getting people out of office, in reality the limitation is put on the voter not the candidate. In creating term limits we voters do nothing more than limit our own foolishness in electing the same people repeatedly. With term limits there is even less incentive to get to know all the candidates and what they stand for because, who cares, they'll be gone next term anyway.

Hey, how about a military coup? We've never done that before. Probably not, what with the military being what it is and all. It would be doubtful they would do it to elevate women to have a serious say on funding and policy. After all military coups are a dime-a-dozen in human history. We need to keep our Americanness about us.

We need to keep our Amerogance, (American Exceptionalism), alive and flourishing the way the American Conservative Union says we should. Who cares if the idea is a bunch of knee-jerk patriotic hokum used to lure the suckers, sorry, constituents to join the party, so they can party on. Just what can we do to breach the two-party monopoly and give Independents and women equal political standing with the two major parties?

Seems we've run out of options. Redoing the Revolution, the Civil War, or term limits won't work. What's left, going French again? Sacre bleu! Yes, there is another French option out there that they have been using, followed by Rwanda and other countries, which has proven successful in expanding the number of women in elected office: quotas.

The problem is, as Dee Dee Myers explained in her book, *Why Women Should Rule the World*, "Such quotas would be impossible in the United States, where policies aimed at increasing representation of women or minorities in public institutions are politically perilous and legally suspect."[84]

Regardless of being perilous or legally suspect the French said oui to 'La Parite' in 2001. By law, any candidate list of any sort had to include the same number of women as men.[85] This from a country where women were not allowed to vote until after we liberated them from Nazi tyranny in 1945. After that time, to Not-See that women should be able to vote, was an unacceptable Not-See point of view. As François Giroud commented in her interview with Geneva Overholser, "I think parity was made necessary because of a pathological misogyny of the political personnel in France."[86] Ms. Overholser observed that, "In Washington dictating parity on ballots would be unimaginable. And talk of pathological misogyny would be political suicide."[87]

That may have been the case in 2001, but a decade later it wasn't a woman who walked up to a male Congressman and shot him in the head at point blank range, it was the other way around. Yes, her good friend and colleague in the House, Congresswoman Debra Wasserman–Shultz is now head of the DNC, but only after her friend was gunned down. Great conciliatory gesture Democrats. Ninety years after women get the right to vote. Strike up the band on that one! Call it what it is, Democratic Party tokenism to appease women in saying we're your party. Who are they fooling? Obviously many women in this country.

Fifty-six years after French women are allowed to vote, they are half the candidates on the ballot, by law, in that country, and

---

[84] Meyers, Dee Dee, Why Women Should Rule the World, Harper-Collins, 2008, p.108.

[85] Overholser, Geneva, French Strike a Blow for Feminism, Seattle Post-Intelligencer, Washington Post Writers Group, April 25, 2001.

[86] Ibid.

[87] Ibid.

they became 40 percent of all local government elected positions. Nah, there's no pathological misogyny in the political system of the land of purple mountains majesty and amber waves of grain. How many more Congresswomen will have to be gunned down before we wake up to the reality of our political culture? *Rwanda woke up.*

Yes, that Rwanda, where 800,000 people were executed during the Rwanda Civil War of 1994. In 2003 they picked up where the French left off by writing a new constitution proclaiming quotas for 30 percent of the seats in Parliament would be women. Again, according to Dee Dee Myers, "But when Rwandan voters went to the polls in October 2003-for the first time since the genocide-they chose more women than the law required."[88]

It didn't stop there. In the Christian Science Monitor's special report on global leadership, they reported that Rwanda made history in 2008 when the country elected women to 56 percent of the seats in Parliament.[89] Another CS Monitor report went on to report that right behind Rwanda with 56.3 percent, were South Africa at 44.5 percent, Cuba at 43.2 percent, followed by Iceland at 42.9 percent of female representation in government.[90]

Former apartheid South Africa, and Fidel's communist Cuba making a mockery of the ossified, out of touch stasis of our political system concerning political equality among men and women. Is this the real reason for the decades long boycott and travel ban for Americans to Cuba? Our political class didn't want us to be influenced by the pinko commie Castro idea of stronger female representation in government compared to our own miserly ways here?

[88] Meyers, Dee Dee, Why Women Should Rule the World, Harper-Collins, 2008, p.109.

[89] http://www.csmonitor.com/World/Global-Issues/2010/1113/Global-leadership-In-Rwanda-women-run-the-show, Christian Science Monitor November 13, 2011.

[90] http://www.csmonitor.com/World/Global-Issues/2010/1113/Global-leadership-Voters-launch-a-power-surge-of-women, Christian Science Monitor November 13, 2011.

Fear not fellow citizens. Hold your heads high Americans! Through good ol' pluck and Amerogance, by way of hard work, fair play and decency, we've ascended the chart of female representation in government to position number 73.[91] Seventy-three! We're right there in a down to the wire photo finish with that land known for its political freedom, equality, and liberty, TurkMENistan!

To show our solidarity with our partner in female representation in government maybe we should do some re-branding to up our profile. How about the United Stans of AMENica? Hey it worked for Blackwater Security, why not us?[92]

With quotas being an accepted method for getting more women into elected office in a variety of countries, would quotas stand a chance here, even after Dee Dee Myers wrote quotas are "impossible," and Geneva Overholser, "unimaginable," in America? This in a country where we have import quotas for anchovies, brooms, ethyl alcohol, olives, milk, cream, tuna, wheat gluten, wire rod, line pipe, blended syrup, upland cotton, chili peppers, dried milk, eggplant, onions, peanuts, watermelon, chocolate, Canadian cheddar cheese; and that's the short list.

Then there are the quotas for commercial fishery catches, quotas for hunting, quotas for trapping game, quotas for the number of people in a legislative district, quotas for irrigation water, immigration quotas, gender quotas, racial quotas, steel quotas, denim quotas, quotas for tires, quotas for tobacco, and of course quotas for mastectomy swimsuits. There is another quota used every day in the good old USA: sales quotas.

---

[91] Ibid.

[92] Disgraced private security contractor in Iraq.

This last item being a standard of performance measured by corporate America in wringing out the maximum amount of work and revenues per employee. It is perfectly okay for corporate America to set sales quotas to increase their market share and profitability, but it's not okay to set ballot or legislative seat quotas to increase women's market share of the political marketplace that would profit the nation greatly in our continued quest for equality? That's right we don't do quotas in America. Quotas are so French, so un-American. According to Supreme Court Justice Sonia Sotomayer it was the quotas of Affirmative Action that helped her in her journey to the Supreme Court.

If we do not promote and accept quotas for women as percentages of names on ballots or seats in the legislative branches of government, as so many other democracies have done following our lead in this form of government, what's left? What's out there that will realize better political equality for Independents and women in our political system? One that will give us an edge, a leg up.

"How about something no one else has tried to do, how about a gender coup?"

"What?"

"Yes, no country has ever done that before, why not us? Why not be the first?"

"A gender coup?"

"Yes."

" What, are you crazy?"

"Yes and..."

"And how then?"

Simple, *all* the female senators of the United States Senate band together and declare their independence from the Democrats and Republicans, thereby creating a third political force in the government. They can put the Democrats and Republicans on notice that if they want to be the majority it will only come about with an Independent women-Democratic majority, or an Independent women-Republican majority. Either way the two-party deadlock in American politics is broken. Broken wide open in revolutionary fashion. The same revolutionary fashion 13 colonies used to break away from the tyranny of British rule in their Declaration of Independence in forming a new political reality. A new political reality that can happen if those women of the Senate remember the words of Thomas Paine, "It is not in numbers, but in unity, that our strength lies."[93]

Hey America, jumping political ship is as American as mom, apple pie, and bad television. James Madison, the ardent Federalist, kicked things off and sided with the anti-Federalists in writing the Bill of Rights. He then went on to run for president as a Republican. During his first term, two ideas of what constituted a Republican came into existence. "From this time on, too, we begin to hear popular mention of the word Democrat. As admiration for France, which had made the word Republican popular, subsided, as Jacobin and Democrat were no longer offensively identical, and further as there were two schools of thought in the Republican ranks, one newer and more aggressive than the other, it became common for the older to designate themselves as Democrats, that is, the true Republicans, the primitive Democrat-Republicans."[94]

Did you notice the Republican-France (Socialist) connection? Are Republicans just closeted, hiding their true nature behind a cloak of faux conservatism? I bet former U.S. Senator Larry Craig of Idaho knows the answer to that one.

---

[93] Paine, Thomas, Common Sense, February 14, 1776, p. 34.

[94] Boyd, James P., Building and Ruling the Republic, Bradley Garretson & Co. 1884, p.475.

The Republican-Socialist alliance continued right along in American history when Ronald Reagan left the Democratic Party for the open arms of the Republican Party in 1962. Reagan is credited with saying he didn't desert the party, the party deserted him. This didn't happen until decades after the New Deal money that helped the Reagan family through the Depression dried up like a desert.[95] Then in 1964, Senator Strom Thurmond D-SC turns Republican. 1989 sees Democrat Texas State representative Rick Perry, and Democrat Louisiana Governor Buddy Roemer, in 1991, do the same.[96]

In 2001, Sen. James Jeffords, R-VT, picked up the ball and bolted from the Republican Party. He took a good look at the *Myway-highway* being built by the Not-Sees of the Great Decider Administration. Then he took the detour to Independentville, and decided lunch with the Democrats was a better balanced meal for Americans politically.

In the same year Mayor Michael Bloomberg, then a Democrat turns Republican. Six years later he turns Independent. In 2006 Senator Joe Lieberman D-CN turns Independent. In 2009 Senator Arlen Specter R-PA turns Democrat, and in December 2012 former Governor Charlie Crist R-FL turns Democrat.[97]

Being deserted by the party is something Sen. Lisa Murkowski of Alaska knows all too well. After Tea Party-and Sarah Palin backed Joe Miller beat her in the Republican primary in the fall of 2010 in Alaska, she ran as a write-in candidate and won back her Senate seat. She of all female senators owes no allegiance to a political party. So, is the idea of all the female senators bolting from their respective parties that outlandish?

[95] Wills, Garry, Reagan's America, Penguin Putnam Group, 2000, Chapter 6, p.76.

[96] The Christian Science Monitor Weekly, Crist's switch draws GOP scorn, December 24, 2012 p. 15.

[97] Ibid.

Let's not forget the women of U.S. House. They have every right to get on the fun too. With our majority rule and minority rights ideals, the females in Congress going Independent would fulfill those ideals. The 40 percent of the voters declaring themselves Independent would now get representation the constitution promotes being the majority of voters. Women too, would get the representation they are constitutionally granted by being the majority. The actions of women in Congress going Independent furthers all the aspects of political change mentioned earlier. The revolutionary aspect, as previously mentioned, and it would reinforce the ideals fought for and won in the Civil War, greater liberty and equality for every American. Such a political move would have repercussions to put it mildly. Let the discussion begin.

The moment the women of Congress would step up to the cameras unified in their declaration of independence from the Democrats and Republicans the world's jaw would drop. China, the land fast becoming the world's economic powerhouse, would be left choking in the dust of our democracy as we hit the Millennium Falcon hyper drive on equality, leaving them in our distant wake, and making their economic miracle look like a second rate magician's trick in need of an upgrade.

Every government would be in shock and awe, and not the phony baloney type of the Great Decider and Deferment Dick. "America's done it again," would be the headlines. The envy of the world would set in again. The envy of people all over the world saying how much they want what we have, and not just for our possessions, but for our freedoms. The freedoms to reinvent the culture and the politics of the country to include more people equally.

More valuable to those who still struggle to attain it, in and out of this country. More valuable than all the iPads ™, iPhones ™, iPods ™, iThis, and iThat the world has ever produced. More valuable than all the declarations of advice being given us in the forms of books like *Strategic Vision*[98], *Time to Start Thinking*[99], and *The World American Made*[100], about America's decline. Better than the essays by Thomas Friedman or Morton Kondrake, about why a third-party presidential candidate will solve all our problems.

They all miss the point by a country mile. No economic or military revival, let alone a third-party Messiah, is going to save the day. Focusing on strengthening and expanding the pursuit of the freedoms of liberty and equality, the ideals we were founded on as a nation, is where our continued success lies. Those political ideals that gave birth to our vast economic and military power. From the nation's inception, our goals have been the pursuit of human freedoms in governance. The self-governance of our individual lives, and self-governance collectively as a nation.

In 1776 we never set out to be the greatest nation economically and militarily the world has ever seen. The Age of Enlightenment gave us loftier pursuits. Our great economic and military power are just the byproducts of these pursuits. Strengthening our resolve to keep pursuing those ideals shining at us, luring us towards the horizon called democracy is where our long-term successes as a nation lies, regardless of the ebb and flow of our economic and military powers. What better way of refining and improving our own freedoms of liberty and equality than by creating the space for women to be on equal footing in the legislative and judicial branches of our

[98] Brzezinski, Zbigniew, Strategic Vision, Basic Books, 2012.

[99] Luce, Edward, Time to Start Thinking, Atlantic Monthly Press, 2012.

[100] Kagan, Robert, The World America Made, Alfred A. Knopf, 2012.

government as men. Creating the space for Independents to be on equal footing with the major parties.

If we wish for the rest of the world to enjoy our freedoms and democracy, refining and improving our own is the most direct path to doing so, and none better than bringing Independent women forward as a third force in our country's governing. By having women equally represented in the legislative and judicial branches of government independent of the Democrats and Republicans, we will have one of the most powerful deterrents to religious extremism both internally and externally.

From the Atlantic drenched shores of western Morocco, continuing eastward across the ancient Roman granaries of Northern Africa, to the mountainous regions of the Afghan-Pakistan border, where it reaches its zenith, the stamp of radical Islam bears its full weight on modern societies. With it comes something else. That something else being a deep and profound fear of women and the power they represent. A fear that is the de facto Achilles heel of radical Islam. A fear that is persistently rendering the followers of such impotent. Impotent to perform in modern cultures where, increasingly, it is women's power that is on the ascent. A man who is unable to perform gets frustrated. That frustration leads to anger, and the anger often turns to violence, sometimes fatal. So much for radical Islam being a mystery to Americans.

So, by giving the 'weaker sex'—a term I use with tongue firmly planted in cheek—equal independent political power, we as a nation become stronger. There is something the current occupants of the Pentagon would do well to dwell on. Dwelling on the idea that women in greater numbers in politics and in the military will strengthen our national security at home and abroad.

Women running the home for so long tells us our domestic stability will be better when they have a greater say in the domestic affairs of the nation. Who better to keep the home(land) operating smoothly with balancing all the personalities, refereeing all the fights, keeping everyone nourished, bathed, healthy, and on time to school than mom?

As Gen. Michael Rose, former head of UN forces in Bosnia has said, "The world will never be a safer place until America abandons its strategy of attempting to spread freedom and democracy around the world by force of military arms."[101]

Interviewed on MSNBC in February 2012 former Republican presidential candidate Jon Huntsman had this to say, "I think we're going to have a problem politically until we get some sort of third-party movement or some alternative voice out there that can put forward new ideas."[102]

The women of the U.S. Senate and U.S. House declaring independence from the two major parties collectively would be that alternative voice to put forth new ideas. Ideas not new to women, but new to the rest of us compared to the stale male way of doing business in the legislative and judicial branches of our government. Ideas that would undoubtedly spawn a new wave of economic movement in the country. With women being able to write and pass legislation to aid the female majority in the workforce, the economic expansion of new businesses to accommodate these new forces will be inevitable.

Tops on the list would be first-rate day care for all children of working mothers. Legislations could be passed offering tax credits and tax rebates for companies setting up onsite professional day care to promote a less stressful working

[101] British General Rose, Michael, The Washington Post, Article and date I cannot remember.

[102] Huntsman, John, Morning Joe, MSNBC, interview with Jon Huntsman, February 22, 2012.

environment for women by knowing their children are in the same building. This would follow one of the basic ideas of Peter Drucker's philosophy on management; creating a work environment for employees that is supportive versus combative in aiding employee productivity. When a working mother only needs to commute to and from work without the added distraction and stress of a separate location for childcare, how much more will this add to her abilities to perform her tasks at work effectively? This is just the tip of the iceberg. Once both mother and child know they will see each other, such as lunch, during the working day, how much less distraction, less stress, will be on that woman when she is at work? The greater productivity by the female employees being less stressed knowing their children are close by will in turn increase the wealth (profit) of the company. Which in turn leads to more taxes being paid that will be offset by the credits or rebates. Such legislation in Washington D.C. speak is known as revenue neutral, not costing the Treasury a dime.

The wealth to American culture? Immeasurable.

Less stressed working mothers are healthier mothers. Less stressed children are healthier children. Healthier mothers and healthier children are less of a burden to the health care system of the country. Done on a national scale, how do you put a value on that?

When the women in the U.S. Senate, the U.S. House, or any state legislative body act out a gender coup they will need our support. The support of the American public and not just those who call themselves Independent voters. If we Americans want change in our political system, we ourselves need to change. Change our ways of thinking to be more accepting of a different way of governing than the current style.

The exceptional behavior by those who wished to create a new form of government centuries ago is what gave birth to the phrase, American Exceptionalism. For that ideal to live on in American democracy, the citizenry must be willing to do exceptional things on a regular basis, politically, to keep the ideal flourishing. There is nothing exceptional about the partisan, polarizing politics on display in America today. You can find that in any democracy, along with the stasis of a two party system.

Are we ready to have Independent women become equal in our government with the in-your-face phony bravado grandstanding that we see so much of today? Are American men up to the task of showing some real strength by getting it up for the idea that Independent women can do the job of governing as well as, and in some cases better than, men? Can women in this country step up to the idea, and accept the responsibility that women can do the job of governing as well as men? If it is openly embraced by the majority of Americans then we are where we think we are in wanting change in our politics and change in our government. If it is met with derision and malice by the majority, then we are not the people collectively we imagine ourselves to be. We would be faced with the reality check that we only talk about change we want, only complain about the change we want in our government. Yes, we could walk the talk, or just continue to squawk, squawk, squawk.

No, I am not proposing anything easy here, in the actions of female legislators declaring, en masse, their party independence, nor you and I being accepting of such action, but what has ever been easy about being American? We all get thrown together into the so-called melting pot, by birth or by choice with all of our humanness intact. Our humanness which often manifests itself like lumps of coal.

Those human lumps of coal named bigotry, misogyny, prejudice, and racism. All of us, myself included, own at least one of these very human qualities. Every day we get up and trudge through our individual lives, in a place where the words, "All men are created equal," are encased in a heavily guarded vacuum sealed container in Independence Hall. Encased in the laws of the nation, the first nation to do so for all the world to see. Words that weigh on our humanity as heavily as those lumps of coal we pack around all day.

So while being bigoted, misogynist, prejudiced, and racist, is being human, to try not to, is being American.

Realize over the last hundred years America has survived World War I, women fighting and earning the right to vote, the foolish prohibition of a drug, a financial depression, repealing the foolish prohibition of a drug, an attack on American soil, another World War, a presidential assassination, the civil rights battles, a botched military invasion into a foreign land, another foolish prohibition of drugs, the removal of the President from office by threat of impeachment, a presidential assassination attempt, twenty percent inflation, another presidential assassination attempt, more horrific budget deficits, another presidential impeachment, another attack on American soil, another botched military invasion into a foreign land, even bigger budget deficits, another financial collapse, and the electing of the first biracial President, yet you think the country couldn't survive the women of the U.S. Senate and the U.S. House declaring their independence politically and being a third force in American politics?
You don't know this country or her people very well do you?

Think again America, about the wave of women on the ascendency, the wave of Independents on the ascendancy, those waves are picking up size and strength every year. You want to get in front of them and try to stop those waves? Go ahead and be my guest. My fellow wave riders and I will be laughing all the way to the beach as we glide by and watch you get pummeled like a sinking ship, the sinking ship of the two-party male majority political system. Surf's Up!

Chapter 4

It is amazing what you can accomplish if you don't care who gets the credit - Harry S. Truman

When the women of the Senate and the House of Representatives do make their move to independence, it won't be enough to be part of the coalition majority. The big changes have been made. Women have real political power, and they will now shape major legislation affecting the lives of us all. This is great stuff, but a problem in the government will still exist. One that is no different today than when the nation was founded. That problem is the way government operates in its day-to-day functioning.

Bureaucracy, that hated word and what it represents. The word people all over the country love to loathe. It is the cause of all our large organizational nightmares, private and public, or so we say. Nations rise and nations fall but it is bureaucracy that never seems to go away. Even when Boris Yeltsin stood on a tank in the midst of the new Russian Revolution the bureaucracy rolled on. What good does it do when you're starting a new nation, like we did, or revolutionizing an existing one, like women in this country can and will, if the way the government operates stays frustratingly the same?

Two hundred plus years ago we may very well have set the globe alight with our own newfangled governmental ideas with the Constitution, Separation of Powers, and Federalism as starting points for new ways to govern, but we did nothing to address new ways of government operation. We followed the path every other form of government before ours did, and continue to do things the Mandarin way. The Mandarin way of government operation that we inherited from our oriental brethren, who developed it over 1000 years ago. The system of government operation laid out according to the flavor of Chinese culture. It's a hierarchal structure that was based very much on the structure of Chinese families, the ruler of which was always the eldest male.[103] Due to age he had the most seniority, and, by Chinese thinking, therefore the most wisdom. The chain of command, as it were, descended in order of the ages of his sons. Each eventually attain ruling power over the family in time due to deaths in the family.

Since that time every form of government, democratic or not, has done the same. If you want to run a government organization, all you needed was to outlast everyone else in that organization. If you want to chair a legislative committee, have the most seniority on that committee and the job is eventually yours. This is how it is. This is how it has been for millennium.

Well, women of America, you're ascending your way to new political heights with your bold move in attaining it, you need something equally bold in changing the way government operates to convince the people of this country you're serious in your endeavors to keep America moving forward toward that horizon.

---

[103] Finer, S.E., History of Government Vol. 1, Book II, No.5 The Formation of the Chinese State, 2. Continuities in Pre-Ch'in China, Oxford University Press, 1997, p. 454-455.

In 1982 while working for the National Park Service, my youthful zeal was in many things I did in life. There I was enjoying another season working in some of the most breathtaking natural scenery in the world.

Back at headquarters, the Head Shed, as we seasonal employees called it, we were calling it another day, and the fine fall day it was. Before me stood the foreman of the radio shop in a tizzy. He was scrambling around asking anyone, and everyone of the maintenance department heads, who needs radios?

After brief the encounter I asked one of my fellow workers what that was all about. He responded by letting me know that the radio shop had an extra $5000 they had yet to spend from this year's budget. If they didn't spend it they'd lose the money in the next year's budget. Business as usual, he said, shaking his head. There was one week left in the government fiscal year and the head of the radio shop was determined to spend that extra $5000 on radios whether anyone needed them or not.

The next day on the trail I couldn't stop thinking about that incident. I started doing the mental math as we hiked in to remove one last suspension bridge for the season. Five thousand dollars in one little shop of one little division, in one National Park. Then I started thinking about all those divisions in all those parks. Then it went further and I started thinking about all those government divisions in every aspect of government including the juggernaut, the Department of Defense. The unspent money being spent on stuff that wasn't needed boggled my own imaginative mind. Is there a better way, I thought to myself? *There is.*

Suppose you own a business and you're looking to balance your budget, this year and every year after. You're looking to save money but you've run out of options. I come along and say I can show you how to save money and for every dollar I help you save, you pay me a one-time 25 cents for each dollar saved. I show you how to save $100,000 annually and you pay me a one-time $25,000. I show you how to save $1 million annually, you pay me $250,000, and so on. Would you take me up on an offer like this? No doubt you would, as there would be no upfront cost to you, and no payment until the savings were realized.

In agreeing to do this do you realize you've just agreed to the terms of revolutionary form of bureaucratic operation initiated in Washington State in 1990? A revolutionary form of operation that was so successful, "The savings to the state went beyond our wildest possible dreams," said the state's Secretary of State Ralph Munro at the time. "What you have to understand is that no other state is close to doing what we are doing. We pave new ground every time we make a move."[104] TIP, Teamwork Incentive Program, was a new idea in government operation.

"In September 1990 employees signed a contract with managers, pledging to use creative new ideas, techniques, and procedures to save the state money."[105]

It was set up to try to close the budget gap at the Department of Social and Health Services, DSHS, with the help of state employees within its Medical Assistance Administration. The team's effort was aimed at private insurance payers who avoided the responsibility to pay for their share of the state's medical assistance cost. Private health insurance companies not wanting to pay what they owe? Sound familiar?

The budgetary shortfall was $36 million and the goal was to collect as much of that amount as possible from the insurer's delinquent underpayments to the state. For every dollar state employees collected above that amount, they would get to keep 25 percent. The state wrote up the contracts in September 1990,

---

[104] Oakland, Mike, The Olympian, p. A1, April 4, 1992.

[105] Ibid.

and 56 DSHS employees sign the contracts with the department managers. State employees in the program now had the same open-ended economic incentives as those in the private sector like Microsoft.

"These sorts of incentives exist in the private sector. We borrowed it from them," said Jim Peterson, assistant secretary for the Medical Assistance Administration. "The private sector clearly uses these kinds of programs to motivate employees."[106]

What happened? The state employees not only hit the $36 million target they trumped it by $9.4 million. In doing so the state employees that signed up were due on average, a $40,000 bonus. Given the incentives, government workers did what private-sector workers do, their job performance rose related to the incentives offered. What did the managers and politicians do? They panicked. Fearing the voter backlash the Washington State government reneged on the contracts they drew up and now refused to pay.

What of the feared voter backlash? It developed, but not the way the department heads and elected officials anticipated. Rather than being upset with the state employees earning huge bonuses, the voters wrath was aimed at those in charge who were attempting to renege on the contracts and not pay. A court battle ensued.

Editorial after editorial from across the political spectrum condemned the department heads and State officials for not living up to their part of the bargain. The State's excuse, presented by the State Productivity Board, SPB, said that the original contracts, the same contract that were approved by the state were, "Vague," and that the team's savings were not carefully monitored despite quarterly reports to the DSHS assistant Sec. Jim Peterson on the team's accomplishments.

[106] Oakland, Mike, The Olympian, p. A1, February 22, 1992.

The state employees did finally settle with a reduced amount per employee. The SPB voted 5–2 to limit all future bonuses at $10,000, effectively killing off the private sector like open-ended compensation to encourage better employee performance.[107]

What did this brief and very successful program teach us? People are people, regardless of being employed as a civil servant or in a private company when it comes to increase job performance as a result of unlimited financial gain. Most people respond to such with more work.

Wait a minute, you say, those good for nothing government employees are paid to do that already. You would be right to say as such, but due to the age-old structure of bureaucracy their motivation is trumped by not rocking the boat, because the only way to excel monetarily is to move up the seniority ladder. When a legitimate detour to that pattern was offered, 56 employees took the detour, and took the state agency to a place no one ever expected.

Stop and think about what these people accomplished with the TIP program. The budgeting process no longer belonged to a few individuals. A chosen few, like department heads, looking to score points with elected officials for more money in next year's budget. The incentive program bypassed legislative budget committees and their chairpersons. Chairpersons usually looking to up their profile and climb the political ladder by offering some smoke and mirrors savings for the taxpayer.

Now take the TIP program in its original form and expand it, and not just in one state agency but all state agencies within a state. Then expanded it even further, to all states. Go further still to the federal level and all federal agencies, and what do you have?

The democratization of bureaucracy.

---

107 Oakland, Mike, The Olympian, p. A1, April 4, 1992.

No longer listening to politically appointed, isolated heads of government agencies pontificating in legislative hearings about what they are doing to streamline the department's functions. No more blowhard legislative committee chairs going on about what they are doing to save Americans financially from the dreaded bureaucratic monster taking over our fair land, and along the way propping up their profile for the next upward move on the political staircase. Now everyone from janitors, secretaries, truck drivers, carpenters, computer programmers, and procurement personnel would have a say in how to more effectively not spend tax dollars based on what they see daily in all jobs and all levels of government.

Who would know better where the money could be saved, Leon Panetta, entrenched D.C. insider and while Secretary of Defense, flew coast-to-coast every weekend at taxpayer expense to "Clear his thinking," or the long term military personnel who have labored away at the same military base for the last 20 years, and who know the nuts and bolts of everyday military purchasing?

So what if the someone in the military becomes a millionaire many times over showing us how to save of millions or billions of dollars annually at their base? Give that person the financial rewards for showing us something entrenched politicians would never have a clue to look for, let alone act on when they did. That elected official is just too busy keeping the money flowing into their district to make sure they are gainfully employed.

The plan could be expanded so that any government employee that would come forward to show that their position is redundant, a cash out would be offered to get them off the government payroll, with incentives such as being able to maintain their government health plan. If they would be willing to sacrifice their government jobs, why should we taxpayers not be willing to sacrifice some near term tax dollars, for the long-term gain of reducing government employee roles?

If this all seems a bit much to bite off at once, fine. Let's try it on a smaller scale. Lesser populated states, with smaller overall government could be the starting place to experiment with these ideas. States like Montana, North Dakota, South Dakota, Wyoming, Vermont, Maine, or Alaska could work and refine such a program to show what would work best on the state level that could go on to the federal level.

No doubt a transfer of wealth would take place moving money from one place to another. That action alone would stir the state and federal monetary pot in healthy ways by getting money moving and flowing.

Interesting to the 1990 Washington State experiment concerning bureaucracy is how it's a marker for one of our current battles, healthcare. Back then private health insurers were shirking their financial commitments to the state, causing a budget shortfall in the DSHS and putting a strain on state health care systems. Twenty-two years later, state governments and private citizens still battle with private health insurers to pay up when they're required to.

The biggest obstacle to initiating a TIP program on the state and federal levels are the entrenched elected officials we often unwisely reelect repeatedly, and longtime department heads whose power would decline in ratio to the number of department employees choosing to go down the new path of open budgeting.

A recent version of the Washington State TIP program is now going on in the Washington D.C. school districts, called Impact Plus. It is a program that allows teachers, who helped their students excel in their learning, become eligible to receive bonuses and higher salaries for their work. The tradeoff for the greater economic rewards for greater work is signing away some job security provisions in their union contracts when they sign up for Impact Plus.[108]

The British have decided to get into the act themselves with a strong desire to reduce welfare rolls. The British government has started a program that will reward government employees, "If they meet specific targets, from reducing truancy and youth crime to getting parents into jobs, the government will pay local authorities up to $6000 per family."[109]

Is Congressman Paul Ryan's spending slashing, political ladder climbing budget, or the current Senate majority leader's special interest stall tactics a better way to save tax dollars than millions of federal employees working to do so with some real financial incentives behind them?

We'll never know until we try.

Should we decide to get the ball rolling on bureaucratic reform, who knows, we could perhaps encourage the private sector to do the same. Just because Washington State took the idea from the private sector doesn't mean this idea couldn't be reapplied there, especially if employees within those companies knew their financial rewards could be just as great. Think of the money Boeing, GE, or GM could save if they let the employees in on the open-ended earnings the top brass always enjoys. Would said companies and their fellow titans of industry and commerce need to spend millions hiring consulting firms to tell them how to be more efficient at what they do? Would such a company need highly paid executives, some excessively so, when the working man or woman the company could show the shareholders what the CEO and the board of directors don't know, because they never set foot in their departments or the

[108] Dillon, Sam, The New York Times, sec 1, p.1, 18, January 1, 2012.

[109] Ridge, Mian, Christian Science Monitor, July 26, 2012.

factory floor, in how to save the company money? Probably not, at least not at the salaries the CEOs and board members are currently making in many companies.

What's wrong with the employees taking their case for economizing directly to the shareholders in return for financial rewards? What's wrong with eliminating the middle man, those overpaid executives, who last an average of five years, to gain access to the wisdom of long-term employees about what is best long-term for the shareholders investment in them, in the company? Nothing is wrong with it except the few bruised executive egos. They should feel lucky that is all they would suffer. Democratizing bureaucracy would have a positive transforming effect in government operations, and on the country as a whole. A transformative effect that would put all government employees on the same budgetary decision-making level as anyone else. Is it not one of our never-ending aims in maintaining democracy to always strive to find ways to bring our great founding blocks of liberty and equality to all aspects of American society including government employment?

Of course it is. Giving government employees the opportunity to gain financially in helping cut government cost, and save tax dollars can only help America become stronger socially and economically.

Yes, it is amazing what you could and can accomplish if you don't care who gets the credit.

Perhaps the best reason for initiating a TIP program at the federal level would be to reduce and eventually eliminate the politics of the budget process. The politics of which both Democrats and Republicans use to build their political power. The financial concerns about the process have taken a back seat to the political grandstanding that hurls the budget process into another world. It is the hyped, pay attention to us, and we're still relevant political posturing that turns a naturally staid crunching of numbers into a grade D Blockbuster minus the special effects. The sooner we get rid of the circus sideshow of political distraction and sleight-of-hand in the budget process, the sooner we can get down to the work of continuing our progress toward more liberty and equality for all Americans.

Chapter 5

God could not be everywhere, therefore he made mothers-
Rudyard Kipling

It is one thing to propose ideas to shake up the status quo in politics, it is a whole different situation to make it happen. Quite possibly the breaking of the two-party rule in America could be the fuse to set off the explosive tension that lies just below the surface in American politics. Who knows, it is reasonable to assume the two-party control may very well be the glue that is presently holding the country together. Getting rid of this may kick off the Balkanization of America, and with it old rivalries between race, religion, and region rearing their ugly heads again. This is not even beginning to approach an even deeper divide that would ensue between men and women, and the age-old dance of who's in power, who is in control between the two.

There is also the weight of history. The history Thomas Payne pointed to in his book Common Sense, "Commerce diminishes the spirit, both the patriotism and military defense. And history sufficiently informs us, that the bravest achievements were always accomplished in the non-age of a nation."[110]

---

[110] Paine, Thomas, Common Sense, February 14, 1776, page 40.

"Youth is the seed time of good habits, as well in nations as in individuals. It might be difficult, if not impossible to form the continent into one government half a century hence. The vast variety of interest, occasioned by an increase of trade and population, would create confusion."[111]

This is what makes it so easy for the politically enterprising moneyed few to distract and divide the population so they are unable to unite to foster widespread change in the political culture. It is also what gives the average citizen a sense of hopelessness in the political world that leads to cynicism and ultimately not participating in democracy at all. Half of us nationally are that way; we don't vote, we don't participate.

Another problem with instituting political change in the manner written in this book is the dangerous nature of doing so. Upset too many well-positioned apples in the political cart and the reaction can and would in some cases be fatal. Let's face it, political and character assassinations have been going on since the early Egyptian kingdoms. The political powers that be may unite together and destroy a third Independent party or candidates, and could unleash a force more harmful to democracy than the semi-coordinated methods that they use today. Methods in their respective lust for power, that run counter to the very principles the nation was founded on in its beginnings. This allows the two major parties to be where they are. A political version of 'Not in my backyard!' Hey we built our political dynasties so everybody else butt out! Democracy and political power is only for Democrats and Republicans, so you political immigrants get lost, and politically lost we are.

For many it is hard to imagine the multitudes in this country getting motivated to do anything. With the majority of Americans struggling with their weight and struggling further

---

[111] Ibid.

122 · *John Marshall*

still to discipline themselves, self-governing not to eat too much, how could anyone in their right mind expect people to discipline themselves concerning anything as extraordinary as supporting radical change in the structure of our government? Let's face it, if the nation won't go on the physical diet to trim its collective waistline, how are you going to motivate these people to go on the fiscal diet to trim the nation's budgetary waistline, let alone supporting advancing women as Independents for greater competition in the politics of the country?

Lethargy, laziness, and complacency are what keep half the population from voting. These traits run the gamut of society. No, it is not something that affects just the poor and the under educated, it is everywhere in our society. Chances are anyone reading this book either knows or is related to someone who doesn't bother to vote. It could be someone like my own father, the former World War II B-24 pilot risking his life in bombing runs over Germany, and running to billionaire Paul Allen the cofounder of Microsoft.

In my father's case he didn't vote because once he started a family his concerns were about supporting his family, so he never registered to vote for fear of being called up on jury duty, and perhaps losing a week or two of income. The fear of jury duty has the same effect on millions of Americans not registering to vote. In Paul Allen's world, in 1998, in the run-up to a special bond election, it was revealed Mr. Allen hadn't bothered to vote in 20 years. He was too busy becoming one of the richest men in the world to be bothered with politically supporting the very democratic system that allowed him to become one. A side note to this is this sorry fact: the state of Washington allowed Mr. Allen to underwrite the entire cost of the bond election. This became the only time in U.S. History that a private citizen paid for the cost of an election. Any guess who's side won?

Be it my own father, or a young computer nerd lusting to be on the *Forbes* wealthiest list, money has distracted so many from maintaining regularly what so many in other parts of the world are being tortured and killed in their pursuit of. Interesting that the loss of monetary wealth over the last four years has caused such a loss of faith by people in this country. A loss of faith no amount of churchgoing and praying to God will replace. How could it? We may very well be a Christian nation, but we are not ruled by the divine laws of God. We are ruled by the laws of man put forth in the Constitution.

The idea that money doesn't make the people but it is people that make the money has been turned completely around in America today. So much so that many now believe they are not what they used to be because they no longer have the financial means or the financial wealth they used to have. That is a sad fact in America today. Sad because so many have let themselves be led to believe that they don't have a value to society, to America, and most importantly to their families and themselves that they used to. They seem to forget that being on the *Forbes* wealthiest list also puts a person on another list, and a dubious one at that, The Most Insecure People in the World List. That's right, Warren Buffett, Bill Gates, Paul Allen, and the Koch Brothers for all their testosterone are also some of the most insecure people in the world. Why else would they have needed to amass such great fortunes if they had already been secure in who and what they are as a person?

Those among us who would profess to know what's good for this country with their tried-and-true methods to restore its luster, to restore the people's faith, are the snake oil merchants and false prophets of our times. As before, no economic, military, or religious revival is going to satisfy what ails us. They are all temporary Band-Aids™ until the next crisis of faith that is brought on by having faith in those limited revivals. A crisis caused in some ways by perhaps only one percent of us having ever bothered to read the Constitution and the Amendments. An hour or two of reading we have never bothered ourselves with. This doesn't even mention knowing our own state constitutions, the laws of the land.

 So the odds are stacked against it all. The mood in much of the country is one of dissolution and anger. Anger because so many understand so little about their government and how it functions. Division is rife in many parts of society. The deck is stacked for the well-connected moneyed few to continue to buy influence over the masses. So does that mean it's time to throw in the towel? Time to say goodbye to dreaming for a better present and better future? Should we succumb to the whims of the self anointed few to rule over everyone? Do we really want to take steps backward in human history and allow a Corporatocracy to rule the day, rule the country?

 Yes, we can all stay willingly ignorant of our history which will help those now in power continue to tighten things up for even more control. Why not? It beats having to get off the couch, cell phone, or computer and having a real conversation with those around us. As long as we are at it, we can ask that many of the freedoms and liberties so many have fought and died for to be removed from everyday life because, well, it's just such a hassle to have to think long and hard about anything these days. Besides there is so much time to be wasted on nothing at all. It used to be that one could fritter one's life away on useless things. Today you can Twitter™ your life away.

 Frittering or twittering, either way it is the age-old symptom of indifference that continues to stupefy so many, so often. What about all those folks in other countries still dreaming, still dying for the day that they can have a say in their own governmental affairs? Who cares! Let them eat cake! If they're lucky enough to be able to have some. Why should we bother giving them hope for something to live for? We fought, we made it, we are here, so what if we want to lazily give it all away in three or four generations? We're Americans and by our divine right it's all right to let it go if we feel like it. Why bother dreaming, scheming, and planning for a better life for ourselves and for future generations? After all we'll all be six feet under in due time, so who cares?

The problem with that way of thinking is that it runs into a great obstacle that it has to yet to overcome in the human spirit. The will to survive. It runs strongest in new life. New life fighting for the chance to continue on, to persevere. A perseverance that is aided by that half of the species who brought that new life into this world, coaxing, prodding, and nurturing the new life along.

They can't help it, they're wired for. Be it a stray dog or cat, an injured bird, a foster child, or a child of their own, women won't give it up. They'd rather not exist than not be able to love. Love something or someone back to health, back to life, or on to a new life that something or someone they love never knew. Yep, they just can't stop themselves and they won't, ever.

Let's face it fellas there is a reality we, as men, cannot escape. "Fundamentally speaking, ...as males, we are the truly superfluous end of the species, useful only for a split second of ecstatic compulsion. We can try to hide this fundamental fact by doting and providing for the families we help make. In fact, the disguise is the reality—men are what they do, nothing more. Women have us beat hands down in the meaning-of-life sweepstakes."[112]

---

112 Boyles, Denis, Rose, Alan, Wellikoff, Alan, and a bunch of other guys,The Modern Man's Guide to Life, Harper and Row, 1987, p.141,142.

So when you have an unhealthy political system within the country whose mental and physical well-being is being stretched to the limit by men acting foolishly in the two party system, who ya gonna call? Ghostbusters?

No, you call on that part of the species that won't give it up. Won't give it up to their last breath. That half of the species that knows in every cell of their bodies that love can do things nothing else can; such as heal that injured bird, keep that dog or cat alive with a good home, help that person who needs encouragement to keep going, or comfort a person they love when ailing. That something that women have flowing through every cell of their beings is that something we have a serious lack of in our politics.

If that power of female love be so great that it creates, nurtures, and sustains all of us into existence, what kind of things could happen to the nation if that power were turned loose on the politics of this nation? A nation commonly referred to in the female form, as in she and her inhabitants, her land, and her ideals. How much longer do we go on fooling ourselves that we can do without women and the power of love that they live and breathe by, as equals in our politics? A power former U.S. Supreme Court Chief Justice John Marshall was well aware of during the beginnings of this nation.

"I have always felt," wrote Marshall, "that national character… depends more on the female part of society than is generally imagined."[113]

Imagine it America. Imagine it until it becomes the reality of our lives in allowing this country to be dependent on politically independent women to help guide and nourish this infant nation. On toward that distant horizon of democracy.

---

113 Smith, Jean Edward, John Marshall, Definer of a Nation, Henry Holt., 1996, p.32.

Epilogue

"If we do not pay for children in good schools, then we are going to pay for them in prisons and mental hospitals."- Eleanor Roosevelt

When I was growing up in northern Illinois, we used to play a game called Find the Blind Spot. You'd stand looking forward, and extend an arm out with your index finger pointing up. Then you'd move your finger across your line of sight, while staring straight ahead, until you found the spot where you couldn't see your finger because of the blind spot in your vision. When I first did it I was amazed that this was possible. I learned at the time that everyone has this spot in their vision. As I learned more about life I came to realize nations have blind spots too. And whatever occupies the blind spot of a nation, that country and its inhabitants can't see the object, the subject clearly. What is one of the things that currently occupies the blind spot in the national vision of America? War. No nation clearly sees war, understands the equation war, until that nation that has defeated, occupied, and ruled over another country and its people has had the same actions put upon themselves. Try as we might in using our self deluding American Exceptionalism as the getaway car against history, against the fate of all nations, history is going catch us. Catch us because most of us will never see it coming right at us from that blind spot. This skewered view is what helps warp our political landscape, and the political warfare we see daily. A political warfare that continues to intensify to the applause of our adversaries. All of whom would love to see this country collapse into civil war between rich and poor, black-and-white, left and right, and/or conservative and liberal so they could come in, pick up the pieces, and reassemble us to their whims. You would think the possibility of such a reality in our future would sober everyone in the country. Sober us up to work together, not fighting amongst ourselves, in particular those in both major parties and elected office. Yet as the current political climate continues to escalate in polarization and partisanship, the only thing that occupies the thinking of the two major parties is grabbing, at any cost, the brass ring of political power.

  Since this book was first published in autumn of 2012 women have made more gains in national office. We now have 20 female U.S. Senators. That is a roughly fifty percent increase from the total in 2005 when we had 13 women in the United States Senate. If that trend continues, by 2023 there will be 30 female senators, and 45 by 2032. At that pace, with a record 104 women currently in both houses of Congress, 18 years from now we would still trail many nations in female legislative representation. When one looks at the speed of change in acceptance of gays in America over the last two decades, the above numbers speak, no, scream loudly to our continued failure to accept women in positions of political power. This state of affairs is as great a stain on American democracy as the racism brought on by this country's failed experiment in slavery in our nation's formative years. That we collectively continue to stumble and trip over a cornerstone of our form of government, majority rule, shows we still have much to learn, and a long way to go in our walk toward the horizon of democracy. Even when pragmatic and sensible examples of our need for more women in the legislative and judicial branches of our government are put before us, we either don't care, or refuse to acknowledge their legitimacy.

No better example of this happened on the floor of the United States Senate in October 2013. There, after the Republican revolt to shut down the government, led by what appeared to be Homer Simpson in the U.S. Senate, Senator Ted Cruz-sader, the most unlikely of outcomes transpired. With all the fire and brimstone heaped upon the American public by one preening, strutting, rhetorical male Congressman after another, female sensibilities prevailed to reopen the government. On the Senate floor stood Sen. John McCain R–AZ, declaring to the American public on C-SPAN, "Leadership, I must fully admit, was provided primarily by women in the Senate."[114] On the heels of this was more of the same by Democratic Sen. Mark Pryor of Arkansas. In speaking about the women of the Senate initiating the legislation to reopen the government, he said, "They allowed us to tag along to see how it's done."[115] Stop for a moment and strip away the party affiliations of both these individuals, and what do you have? Two men, veterans of countless legislative battles and stalemates, telling us the women of the Senate can accomplish what their male counterparts could not do, because those men collectively lacked the political testicles to make it happen. Congressional male members with no testicles! No wonder Congress can't get it up to produce the goods in keeping the country moving forward and evolving. What other current political stalemate could come to an end if women were allowed to be the architects of the legislation to end the conflict? Where in recent American history have we been given a clearer example

---

[114] http://www.nationaljournal.com/congress/male-senators-begrudgingly-admit-women-are-important-20131016

[115] ibid

that women are better at the job of creating legislation that can pass muster with the majority of their colleagues than this?

 This effort, this action, by the women in the Senate was still clearly visible when it came time for the current Democratic Governor of Montana to decide who to appoint to the newly vacated Senate seat by former U.S. Senator Max Baucus in early 2014. The fact that Governor Bullock would appoint his Lieutenant Governor., John Walsh, shows how stuck in the past the hierarchy of the Democratic Party is. The party's desire to *hold onto* old power, by appointing a military man rather than *create* new power by appointing a woman to the U.S. Senate reveals Democratic party power mongering at its worst. Immediately after former Senator Max Baucus announced his intention to retire, a Democratic Senatorial candidate, Dirk Adams, called upon the governor to appoint a woman. His pleas went unacknowledged by the tone deaf ears of party officials nationally and in the state of Montana. Those tone deaf ears paid the price when the New York Times revealed Senator Walsh's plagiarism of his Master's thesis, causing him to drop out of the running for the senate seat he held. The party then tapped State Rep. Amanda Curtis, D-Butte, a Montana political Youtube sensation, to take his place. It was too little too late. U.S. Rep Steve Daines R-MT, who voted in favor of the government shutdown, became the new U.S. Senator from Montana, D'oh!

  Call it misogyny, call it bigotry, call it what you will, the fact is those very human qualities got in the way during the decision about whether to appoint a woman to the United States Senate to represent the people of Montana. The problem with those very human qualities mentioned earlier, (**p.107**), of bigotry, misogyny, prejudice, and racism, left unchecked, they become training camps along the road to authoritarian rule, something no major political party is immune to. For when a political party has the opportunity to appoint a member of the majority, that in population and workforce, to position of true political power and refused to do so, they reveal their very undemocratic thinking and motivations for all to see. To see that political power is more important for the two major parties than the very system of governing that allowed those parties to achieve power in the first place, reinforces everything stated in this book of how the two major parties are crippling America's version of democracy.

As to those female senators who were helping reopen the government? They get together regularly to meet, talk, and exchange ideas. They put party politics aside during those informal chats, just as they did to reopen the government shutdown. When are the rest of the women in this country going to do the same, putting their political differences aside, and sit down, and have regular conversations? Conversations with women they perceive, perceived being the key word, to be so different from themselves that they believe have little or nothing in common because of the liberal/conservative, Democrat/ Republican shell game they buy into. A shell game that will never change until we in America are willing to create new political dialogue in this country. A political dialogue that also reflects what women want, what women need to help run the country. The kind of dialogue that includes what women say to one another with no men around. The kind of dialogue that includes what women say to the children they bore, and the grandchildren they adore. Yes, the political dialogue needs to change from; throw your hat in the ring, build up your war chest, and be ready to take enemy fire from your opposition, because politics is a blood sport. As the late Mario Coumo stated years ago, "there is a subtext of male violence in American politics."[116] This was fine when overambitious males were all that existed in politics, but it's not that way anymore. Anymore than we can think we can ignore or deny the inevitable tides of change happening in our country concerning women and our real need for their influence in running the country.

Since this book was first published this individual did something no one ever thought of attempting, let alone doing on American soil; proposing an initiative to amend a state Constitution to make the legislature fifty percent men and fifty percent women. CI–114 made the cut through Montana Legislative Legal Services, the Montana Attorney General's office, and the Secretary of State's office to qualify for the collection of signatures in an attempt to make the November 2014 ballot. I stated my case to the citizens of the state in the spring of 2014 with the following:

"One hundred years ago in Montana a great discussion, as great as the state itself, was taking place. To the citizens of the state was put forth the idea that women should have the right to vote. The state had been in existence for 25 years, and the nation a century longer, yet women were considered less qualified than former slaves in having a say electing those to public office. By the end of Election Day 1914, the majority of men decided on the side of liberty and equality, and gave the women of the state the right to vote six years before it would become federal law. In the first election where women were allowed to vote, Montanans challenged themselves and the nation in revolutionary fashion by electing the first woman, Jeanette Rankin, to the U.S. Congress in 1916. One hundred years later the female descendants of those Montanans along with the state's never ending flow of female immigrants into the state, have become

---

[116] Freedland, Jonathan, Hillary Clinton must face down ageism, Guardian Weekly, January 15, 2015 P.19, http://www.theguardian.com/commentisfree/2015/jan/02/hillary-clinton-old-woman-white-house-2016-america

half the state's population and workforce. Yet sadly, due to the increasing viciousness of today's hostile, combative, and faux battlefield campaigning process, women continue to be put off in pursuing public office.

To counter this, and the deficit of women in the Montana legislature, I have proposed nothing more or less revolutionary than allowing women the right to vote; asking the citizens of Montana to amend our Constitution to provide that half the legislative seats be for women. Isn't it time the legislature reflected the population and the work force? Isn't it time we create the discussion and a place for all of those well qualified women in the state to help represent us? CI-114 proposes just that in allowing the citizens of the state the opportunity to transform and restructure our government, and along the way for the citizens of Montana to discuss among ourselves why we have so few female legislators, and how we can achieve parity among men and women in our legislature to mirror our state's population.

To those who would ask how and why I came up with such a proposal, in a word, you. You the citizens of this state helped create CI-114. A proposal born of the knowledge gained watching what you do. What have I been watching? Watching the number of Montana girls, year after year, graduating from high school with top honors, sometimes two to one and three to one, over the boys graduating. Why is this happening? Parents doing what parents always do; encouraging their children to excel in life in the hopes of attaining a better life than they themselves have. In Montana along with the rest of the nation, the girls are leading the way graduating with top high school honors, entering college, and graduating from college. Be it Sidney or Noxon, Billings or Missoula, Democrat or Republican, conservative or liberal, this trend of females excelling crosses all affiliations, and all boundaries. Why? Because a parent's love for their children knows no boundaries.

Now take this trend and project it out two decades and what do you have? Thousands if not tens of thousands of more young women with college degrees than men in the state. How are we going to keep all these highly educated women, and the potential families they would help create and sustain from leaving the state and going elsewhere? One way will be to create a political environment that encourages women to participate in greater numbers than they do now. A political environment that acknowledges that democracy in Montana will never reach its full potential until women are in equal numbers as men in representing the population.

To the detractors and critics of CI-114 I say this; come up with a better proposal. Come up with a better idea. One that will promote in even greater terms, getting more women on the ballot, and in the Montana Legislature. One that will offer greater hope of our legislature mirroring our population for future generations of Montanans. I hope you will support CI-114 by signing a petition, and continuing the discussion this state is ready to have."[117]

My lack of understanding the signature gathering process is what kept this idea from coming to fruition. Now understanding what it will take in money, people, and time to make it happen, all the better for the next attempt. Taking this to the citizens of the state that has the second least amended State Constitution in the nation is pushing uphill all the way. Uphill? Love going uphill. Steep, craggy, a long way off? Hey when do we start? This is Montana after all, and if you don't enjoy long, steep, and

[117] Marshall, John, The Daily Interlake April 6, 2014 Sec D, page 2, http://missoulian.com/news/opinion/columnists/support-mandate-for-more-women-in-legislature/article_645cef42-caf3-11e3-8773-0014abcf887a.html, April 23, 2014.

uphill, or going it alone down a path rarely travelled, or no path at all, this isn't the place for you. This writer is right at home here, be it in the thick of unexplored wilderness, or the the thick of the political wilderness. Let's go!

In March 2013 while attending the Dent the Future conference in Ketchum, Idaho I had a wonderful conversation with the irrepressible Sunny Bates, the mentor, mother, and muse behind the crowd source funding phenomena, Kickstarter. I asked her what she thought it would take to get women in equal numbers in the legislative branches of American government.

"That's a good question," she responded, "I was at a conference recently and in the room were probably 180 of the most powerful women in America. We were there to listen the Liberian women's activist Leymah Gbowee. She had just won the Nobel Prize. She was standing there telling all of us to stand up for our rights. She was talking about the comment made by Republican Foster Friess about women holding aspirin between their knees as a contraceptive. She said, 'How dare you let any man, any politician speak to you like this. How dare you let anyone speak about you in this way and get away with it. The entire world is watching you, women and men. They are watching what you do. If you cannot stand up for yourselves they will see this, and it will be harder for women everywhere to stand up to these people.'" Sunny continued, "She spoke with such power, such force, that we all felt ashamed." When I asked if anything had come out of that speech Sunny responded,"Not what I or most of these women had hoped."

To those 180 women who were in that room what are you waiting for? What are you afraid of? Women created all of us. Women own us. When are you going to stand up, united, against this kind of talk and behavior? Stand up for your rightful place in this country politically? Cheryl Sandberg wrote a book titled,

Lean In. Great. Within a year of publishing her bestseller, Ms. Sandberg leaned in the direction of the mostly male corporate board (7 out of 10), in backing a new maternity policy at Facebook. Facebook will pay the cost for female employees to freeze their eggs to postpone childbirth, rather than establish company wide maternity leave and on site child care. Perhaps freezing Mark Zuckerberg's testicles, and that of the Facebook board's male members is a better way to go. A better way to go until they wake up to the emptiness of their flaccid maternity policy.

When are the likes of the Ms. Sandbergs of this country going to Lean In the direction of the waitresses, maids, cooks, childcare workers, etc., and work politically to help them get where she is? Where is Oprah when the women in this country truly need her? She has the fab Zine, the lifestyle, and the billions in net worth, but what is it all worth if she can't help the women she used to be? She likes to give away cars, I wonder if she's ever thought about focusing her power in the form of time, money, and her super savvy media skills, and go nationwide on a treasure hunt. A treasure hunt to find, cultivate, and present female candidates at all levels of public office to go toe to toe with the big boys? She didn't blink when the big bad boys of the beef industry challenged her, why let the big bad boys of the Democratic and Republican parties off the hook so easily?

After speaking to women from all walks of life and all different ages in the last two years, I can see clearly that the main obstacle to getting women in equal numbers in elected office is women themselves. A comment often brought up by women in this country is raising a family. Raising kids consumes so much of their lives they say that they have no time for politics,. Funny, in the two Canadian Provinces that border my home state, both have Premiers that are working mothers. In the province of

British Columbia, Provincial Premier Christy Clark is a single working mother with two children. Are Canadian women that far superior to women in this country? I doubt it. With all the women in this country I've spoken with, none have a plausible explanation as to why women in other countries have been able to accomplish what American women have not. It all comes down to self respect, believing in themselves. This is what keeps women, collectively, from the reigns of political power.

Time has shown some of the causes that contribute to this; the de-feminizing of women in American culture starting at an early age, and our inability to see the dangers that monotheistic and patriarchal religions can have on an all inclusive democratic system of governing. On the first point, go watch girls high school sports and what do you see? The high fives, fist bumps, surfer dude hand signs, you name it, are all coming from the male side of American sports culture. Why do they try to emulate the boys in sports? Because culturally we promote it and support it. We guys want them to be more like us so we don't feel vulnerable around them, and we can stay safely ensconced in our worlds thinking we have the upper hand, when ultimately we don't. On the second point, the birth of monotheistic religion, paternal for Judaism, Christianity, and Islam, was also the birth of religious intolerance. One male God to worship, to believe in, and one way to do so. Sorry gals, you've just been relegated to the back of the humanity bus. Try as we might to keep all forms of worship open and unfettered, along with keeping them out of the governing of our lives in America, their millenniums old influence on humanity still bends us away from the democratic principles set forth in the U.S. Constitution. Bends us away from the idea, made the law of the land through our Constitution, that constitutionally, politically, and in government, women are equal to men, regardless what accepted western religious texts say to the contrary.

This brings about the need for a very simple statement. A statement this writer made as a Republican candidate for the U.S. Senate in Washington State at an open candidate forum assembled in a church in October 1998, "The Good Book, the Bible, educates us about the power of the Almighty and all that power can do for mankind, yet it is the Great Book, The Constitution of The United States of America that educates us about the almighty power of the people, still the absolute authority in all the affairs of governing the people in the country. And it can be said with certainty that if that Great Book, The Constitution did not exist, all of the religious Good Books of the world would not be allowed to be practiced, preached, and spoken so openly, so freely in America if that Great Book did not exist." Unfortunately many American's view of religion is void, willfully so, of this very important fact. Those Americans that are are blissfully ignorant. An ignorance that continue to grow in this country, and justifies being against or for something regardless of whether or not it passes the constitutional test, for the sole purpose of reinforcing ones personal religious beliefs. We just haven't been around long enough as a people, as a country, for many to grasp what others in older nations have; the dangers of letting religious dogma supplant constitutional pragmatism pertaining to liberty and equality.

Since times immortal we humans have elected and anointed our gods. Gods we appoint and anoint to *lead* us to salvation. We are now unconsciously projecting the same on our elected representatives that they *lead* us, lead us to the political promised land. If they tell us they will, the deification process starts, and we bestow unrealistic godlike qualities upon them. If they don't, their fall from political grace is swift. Be it Hillary Clinton or

Senator Elizabeth Warren on the Democratic side, or Jeb Bush or Senator Ted Cruz-sader on the Republican side, we project our desire to be led. This topic will be discussed at length in the next book.

Paul Kane writing for the Washington Post summed up Senator Warren's popularity this way, "But the crowd roared its approval for Warren, whose challenges to the banking industry have turned her into an icon less than two years into her first term."[118] She is no longer a woman, mother, or Senator. She is viewed by many as an icon. How did she attain this? Simple, there are not enough men in the Senate, with her concerns for the average American to speak up, and pass legislation to put the big banks and Wall Street on a short tight leash. The men we elect won't do it. They're doing exactly what The Great Philanderer did (p.86), putting on their senatorial knee pads, and opening wide to service big money. Unfortunately some women in positions of political power are aping their male colleagues to the detriment off all women, of all Americans.

The earlier quote by Eleanor Roosevelt reveals the foolishness in this kind of thinking, this kind of activity. Collectively for women in America today, it will require walking in the footsteps, literally, with the same loud voices, the same regular protesting, and the same sacrifices made by women in the suffrage movement a century ago to get where they want to be politically today and in the future. The national child care plan mentioned in Chapter Three, and a similar plan put forth by The Great Yes We Can in his 2015 State of the Union message can come sooner than later when the silent majority is silent no more. When half the work force in this country, women, walk off their jobs en mass, and take to the streets demanding it become law, it will.

[118] Kane, Paul, http://www.washingtonpost.com/politics/2014/10/24/48765a5e-5660-11e4-809b-8cc0a295c773_story.html, Washington Post, October 24, 2014

What better way to pay for children's good schooling to keep them out of prisons and mental hospitals, than having them watch their mothers, their grandmothers, and their aunts along with their fathers, grandfathers, and uncles protesting loudly, peacefully, in the streets of America standing up for *their* rights, for *their* future.